**YOUR
SPIRITUAL
JOURNEY**
*A Guide to the River
of Life*

D0533229

Ruth White is a highly respected spiritual teacher who runs a counselling practice and workshops in the UK, Russia and many European countries. She has worked as a channel for guidance from Gildas for many years. Her other books include *Gildas Communicates*, *Seven Inner Journeys*, *The Healing Spectrum*, *A Question of Guidance*, *Working With Your Chakras* (Piatkus), *Chakras: A New Approach to Healing Your Life* (Piatkus) and *A Message of Love* (Piatkus).

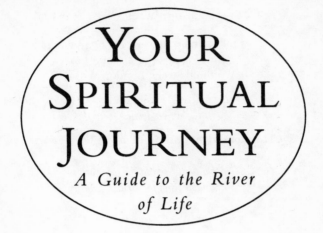

YOUR SPIRITUAL JOURNEY

A Guide to the River of Life

RUTH WHITE

PIATKUS

First published in 1995 as *The River of Life* by
Judy Piatkus (Publishers) Ltd
5 Windmill Street, London W1P 1HF

This edition published in 1998

The moral right of the author has been asserted

*A catalogue record for this book is
available from the British Library*

ISBN 0-7499-1903-5

Edited by Esther Jagger
Designed by Sue Ryall

Set in 12/14pt Monophoto Baskerville by
Datix International Limited, Bungay, Suffolk
Printed in Great Britain by
Biddles Ltd, Guildford & King's Lynn

To my daughter, Jane

Acknowledgements

The people who attend my workshops provide the inspiration for the development of the guided journeys.

My close friends stay friends, even when I am non-communicative because all I can think about is writing.

My daughter, Jane, is a tremendous support and confidante in all I do. She drew the diagrams in this book.

Tony Van den Bergh has read the manuscript and offered suggestions at every stage with patience, love and humour.

My dog, Jackson, has sat faithfully on my feet, keeping me company during many hours of typing.

My publishers never seem to lose faith or patience, even when I am doubtful about deadlines.

To all of you, my love and thanks.

Contents

Prologue

'I have trodden the vineyard alone'
OLD TESTAMENT: Book of Jeremiah

Personal History

I was born in Bournville, Birmingham in 1938, the year before the Second World War was declared. The peace of life in the famous 'garden village' was disrupted, as it was everywhere. Anderson shelters were dug in at the ends of our gardens, gas masks issued and blackout curtains drawn. I was old enough by then to have a Mickey Mouse gas mask, red in colour and with a long wobbly tongue designed to make it less frightening to wear. Smaller babies were put into contraptions rather like incubators during air raids, while adults carried the square boxes containing their masks wherever they went.

I remember being woken from sleep by the wail of the siren. Anxious about making the trek to the shelter at the bottom of the garden, my mother and father made a bed for us all behind the piano, next to the warmth of the chimney breast. A land mine dropped quite near to the shelter we had avoided. Next morning we went to see the huge crater it had made.

My father was a pacifist and conscientious objector, but by agreeing to do some 'war work' he escaped imprisonment. His and my mother's task was to look after evacuees in a requisitioned Warwickshire country house. In addition my father supervised the running of two farms where the labourers were Italian prisoners of war. Unable to pronounce the 'th' at the end of my Christian name, they christened me 'Rosa'.

Flower fairies, tree spirits, angels and guides

The country house had extensive gardens and the farms covered a large acreage. So in war-torn Britain I spent my early years in a country environment. Wandering across once-gracious lawns, through neglected shrubberies and into the fields, I was never alone. I could see the flower fairies and tree spirits and was accompanied by a shining being dressed in white. Having learned about angels from a Bible picture book, I presumed this masculine presence to be my personal angel. I felt safe when he was near and conversed freely with him. I only had to think of him and he was there beside me. I also began to see colours around people, and often spoke about them.

For a while my references to these things were 'humoured'. It certainly did not occur to me that others were not seeing what I saw. But after a while my parents decided that I was too introspective and began to punish me for my 'fantasies and lies'. I learned to keep my experiences to myself, but still enjoyed my garden and field walks with all the additional life I could see and with which I could converse.

Later, as the war continued, we went back to Bournville. Cadbury's were producing essential supplies for the troops and my father worked there, servicing the steam locomotives on the railway which ran right into the factory grounds. As I grew older, my parents became more harsh with me. They wanted me to be perfect and had very set ideas about what perfection entailed.

I tried hard to understand what was required of me, and became frightened of my own inner world. By the time I was fourteen I was so confused by denying my own experiences that I could see neither within nor without. I repressed all my early childhood memories and was very lonely.

A school eye specialist told my parents that I was going blind and would need to be transferred to a school for the partially sighted. Although this did not actually take place, my school work and reading were severely restricted. I was interested in languages and wanted to be an interpreter, but I was advised to do something more practical like market gardening. Somehow it was decided that I should teach nursery school children and, still completely confused, I went off to the City of Leicester training college.

My first exposure to a class of nursery-age children threatened to escalate a complete nervous breakdown. Leicester was the only college in the country at that time to offer counselling. I was advised to see Dr Mary Swainson, who was not only a Jungian therapist but an inner brother of the White Eagle Lodge and thus had deep esoteric knowledge. Slowly I realised that here, at last, was someone who understood. Mary recognised my experiences and validated them.

Gradually my inner world re-established itself. I learned that my 'angel' was actually a discarnate guide called Gildas (these and other specialised terms are explained in the Glossary). I was nineteen years old when I began to 'channel' teachings from this radiant being. During the long years of psychological and spiritual work which enabled me to establish the relationship with Gildas which I have today, he was, and remains, constantly by my side.

The development of my present work

I went on to teach young children, to marry, to give birth to Jane, my daughter, and to divorce. Eventually I established the range of work with which I am involved today. I am a trained counsellor, I am a writer, and I channel teachings from Gildas for general information, to help individuals with problem areas of life and for use in my books. I use my teaching experience to help me in the running of workshops for healers and those interested in 'spiritual growth'.

Gildas

My guide, Gildas, has told me only a little about himself. His last incarnation was as a monk in fourteenth-century France. Since then, he has become part of a large group of teachers on the 'other side' who are seeking to help humanity by communicating the wider perspective to life which they are able to see from that other dimension. He has gone through the evolutionary requirements of incarnation and will probably not choose to incarnate again.

As I did when I was a child, I only have to think of Gildas and he is beside me. The shining white presence who was my 'angel' I now know as a being of light wearing white monk's robes. As time goes by I see him less often as a being and more often in his energy body, which is a pattern of light and colour.

I hear his communication like dictation. For many years I always wrote it down. Now I still hear it in the same way, but usually speak what I am hearing into a tape recorder.

Gildas has helped me to establish my spiritual belief

system, which includes belief in past lives, karma and reincarnation. His earliest teaching was about the way the 'jewel of truth' has many facets. At any given time or from most angles of perception we can see only a proportion of these facets. Spirituality and religion often get caught up too much in dogma and 'either/or' black and white perspectives. We are gifted, as a whole, with an innate sense of what is 'of good report'. True tolerance comes from the 'and/and' position and the recognition that there are many shades of grey. This gives less security and has complacency as its danger. Yet only from here can we really enjoy the vast richness of our differences. This is the path of wholeness as opposed to the path of perfection. To tread it we need to cultivate a fine discernment. It leads to spiritual growth, co-creatorship and personal empowerment.

A golden age on earth

Gildas and other discarnate guides see their task as one of helping us to prepare for a 'golden age' on earth. They tell us that it is coming soon. They are not pessimistic about the present state of our world. 'A quantum leap in consciousness' is due to be made in the next forty to fifty years. We may often feel that the little we can contribute as individuals is but a drop in the ocean. Yet the guides assure us that the main way in which we can help is by working on ourselves to attain a self-knowledge which includes, but transcends, ordinary psychological insights. Such knowledge allows the flame of the true spirit which resides in each one of us to shine through. It also enables us to perceive the spark of that flame in each other and to celebrate our common spirituality.

1

From the Source to the Sea

We shall not cease from exploration
And the end of all our exploring
Will be to arrive where we started
And know the place for the first time.
T.S. ELIOT: Four Quartets

Visualisation . . . Spiritual and psychological exploration . . .
Gildas . . . Guided journeys . . .

Visualisation

'Visualise a river, flowing from its source to the sea.
Imagine it as the river of your life . . .' Having read these
words you might already have a picture of a river in
your mind's eye. This river may have features of rivers
that you have actually seen, where you have rowed,
punted, sailed, fished or sat beside lush green and flowery
banks to read or dream. Yet because this river in your
mind's eye is being seen as 'the river of your life' it is also
a part of your inner landscape. As such it will be unique.
The familiar rivers of the outer world are contained
within it but this waterway is yours, symbolically repre-
senting the journey of your life with all its delights,
discomforts, dreams and disappointments – a thrilling
chimera of memory and potential.

If you find visualisation difficult, the phrase 'river of

life' can still inspire a flow of reminiscence and thought. It can be a creative exploration of past joys and chagrins, future hopes and fears.

The source of a river may begin with droplets of water gradually welling to a stream. Similarly, the memories of babyhood and very early childhood are usually scattered and intermittent, whilst the later years of youth evoke a more steady flow of recollection. We all tend to live a little in the past and/or future as well as in the present. Mighty rivers flow to the sea. Do the droplets emerging from the source know their destiny? Are those same droplets contained in the flow which we watch as we stand at a river's edge? Have they been changed as a result of their journey so far? Will they change again as they move on? Will a continuing essence be carried from the source to the sea?

If the river signifies the journey of life, the sea may represent the end of that voyage. Within the present symbolism it may be seen variously as adulthood, the accumulation of the contributions which each individual makes to the whole, death, or the collective unconscious.

Spiritual As Well As Psychological Exploration

Watching an actual or imaginary river flowing from its source, making the journey through varied territory to an eventual meeting with the sea, evokes more than an exploration of memories related to the mental, physical and emotional journey through life. The very word 'source' has spiritual connotations and calls forth some of the eternally fascinating questions: 'Who am I?', 'Where do I come from?', 'Where and how does my journey end?', 'What is my destiny or purpose?', 'Who decides it and how do I accomplish it?'

Such matters have been called 'the imponderables of life'. They can never be answered with conclusive or objective proof. Yet we ponder them just the same. In all ages there are those who pursue a higher meaning or purpose in living. An increasing number of people today are experiencing a discontent at being 'normal' – the downside of this during the present years of recession is the growth of criminality. Its positive aspect is reflected in the increasing demand for self-knowledge and the eagerness to explore fully the boundaries of human potential. This has become a 'growth industry' in every sense.

We need to be able to explore with greater confidence. We need to find at least a working hypothesis on a broad-based spiritual front in order to meet creatively the challenges with which we are confronted by life. Conventional religions with their dogmatic frameworks offer only limited signposts for many aspirants. Psycho-analysis and long-term psychotherapy are the privileges of the few.

My aim in the following pages is to inspire deeper examination of issues related to spiritual growth as well as to help in the cultivation of those skills and inner resources which form a safe backdrop to creative self-exploration.

Gildas

My discarnate guide, known and loved as Gildas, has given teachings on a number of 'key-words for spiritual growth', and extracts from these will form a part of each chapter.

Guided Journeys and Exercises

There are guided meditations and suggestions for exercises at each stage of the investigation. Each inner journey takes as its theme some aspect of the river of life.

For guided journeys you need to achieve that state of relaxation which allows an alert creativity. Your body should be comfortable without being floppy. Before undertaking the exercises in this book decide what is the best place in the house and the best time of day for you to be mentally, as well as physically, relaxed and receptive. It is difficult to achieve a good inner flow if you are worried about an expected (or unexpected) phone call or if children's needs or other concerns may impinge on your space. Switch the phone off. Be sure that everyone knows that you are not to be disturbed. Making these arrangements is, in itself, an exercise in self-value and has a bearing on your commitment to your process of self-growth.

Some people can only journey inwardly if they are lying down; others find that lying down is their signal to go to sleep. Experiment to find what is best for you but, whether sitting or lying, your body should be symmetrically arranged. Cross-legged or lotus postures are fine, but if you are lying down or sitting in a comfortable chair, your legs should not be crossed at the knees or ankles. This is because there are electrical 'circuits' in and around the body. Symmetrical positions keep these circuits open; other positions may block them and inhibit the flow of what you are aiming to achieve.

Always read through and make sure you understand each exercise or guided journey before you begin to work with it. You may also like to read the guided journeys on to tape before you follow them. It takes only a little practice to record them at a pleasant working pace. It is a good idea to have paper, pens, pencils and paints or coloured crayons nearby for recording your journeys, thoughts, realisations and conclusions.

Basic Thematic Journey: The River of Life

Making sure that you will be undisturbed, find a comfortable, supported and symmetrical position in which to sit or lie. Become aware of the rhythm of your breathing and focus this into the centre of your body on a level with your physical heart. (This is your heart centre or chakra.) Thus activating your heart energy, enter your inner space and find yourself in a meadow . . . activate your inner senses so that you see the objects and colours . . . you hear the sounds . . . you touch the textures . . . you taste the tastes . . . you smell the fragrances . . .

Within or beyond the meadow, a river runs through your inner landscape . . . As you begin to make your way towards it, notice how you are dressed for the journey . . . Call for any companion you would like to accompany you (maybe an animal friend or an inner wise presence) . . . Take with you any symbolic object, amulet or talisman which you know brings you a sense of protection and helps you to be 'centred'(See Chapter 2).

When you feel ready, make your way towards the river and find a comfortable, warm place where you can sit and observe its flow . . . This is the river of your life . . . Gradually, on a number of occasions, you are going to explore it . . . but now just sit and contemplate it and the area where you have joined it . . . Notice the colour of the water . . . the speed of its flow . . . the width of the river . . . the state of its banks . . . Are they steep or

gently sloping . . . ? Is there plant life on the banks . . . ?
In the river . . . are fish to be found here . . . ? Is there
any 'traffic' on your river . . . ? Be aware that the river
originated at a source and will, even if it is a tributary
to a larger river, flow on to the sea . . . How do you feel
about this river . . . ? Are you excited to think about
exploring it further?

Stay here, without moving further along the river in
either direction, for up to a further fifteen minutes, but
then return to your meadow . . . to the rhythm of your
breathing in your heart centre . . . to an awareness of
your body and of your contact with the ground, sofa or
chair . . . Open your eyes and return to your normal
surroundings . . . Take pens, pencils, paints, colours and
paper to record your journey and your responses to the
questions which were posed.

2

Time and Tide

Resolve to be thyself: and know, that he
Who finds himself, loses his misery.

MATTHEW ARNOLD

*The art of meditation and making guided journeys . . . The
interface between psychological and spiritual work . . . Keeping a river of life workbook . . . Some notes on symbolism
. . . Some of the most frequent questions asked or fears
expressed about visualisation*

Starting Meditation and
Guided Journeys

Advice about ensuring that you will be uninterrupted
when you wish to do work of a psychological or spiritual
nature has already been given (see page 10). There are
also other factors and guidelines to consider before you
begin. Even if you are not a 'natural', the art of inner
exploration can be developed with time and patience.
Knowing and observing some simple and sensible guidelines will ensure that you remain in charge and therefore
never experience the 'flip side' of inner journeying.

Time and Discipline

Some people hesitate to undertake 'inner work' because of time pressures, or perhaps because they associate meditation with discipline – and discipline deters many of us. A first look at this book, with its theme of an extended journey, could give a sense of being faced with too great a challenge. When considering an undertaking connected with self-knowledge and spiritual development, it is important not to build in a structure which leads to a sense of failure or diminution of self. The goal of self-knowledge is positive: its aim is to enhance self-esteem and to enable creative living.

The Pitfalls of Goal-Setting

Many of us may encounter unexpected pitfalls in our desire to set goals, to have clearly defined targets and to measure achievement. We live in a goal-orientated, action-worshipping, competitive world. Inner and spiritual exploration should be a joy and an increment unencumbered by self-judgemental attitudes to discipline and performance. So before you begin, determine that every part of the journey you undertake, every moment of time you manage to set aside, every symbol you receive, is to be embraced as a precious gift. How often, how long or how many does not matter. The nature of guided journeys and the power of symbols within the psyche is that they awaken a flow which continues. The pull of outer world commitments and the spaces in between the times of self-communion do not dam this flow.

The inner landscape, unless entirely neglected,

suppressed or devalued, goes on producing riches to be joyfully discovered whenever we are ready. The process should never be forced. Too much pressure or expectation renders the psyche resistant or defensive. Establish a rhythm which is comfortable and manageable alongside the other commitments in your life. Your respect for the inner dimension will enable the journey to unfold. Try not to make demands on yourself which are phrased along the lines of: 'Every Thursday at 2pm I will religiously set aside time for this work.' Whilst it is good to note the days when you are likely to be able to take time for your journey, there should be no rigid expectations. The day will inevitably come when you fail to meet your appointment with yourself, and a 'failure seed' may then be sown. If you take the attitude that each piece of inner work accomplished, no matter how small, is a happy achievement, you will be sowing the seeds of success. In this way the regularity of self-work will grow for positive reasons and not from a rigorously imposed or artificial discipline.

Meditation

Confusion frequently arises as to what meditation is and our expectations of it. Once commonly practised only in oriental religions, meditation has become increasingly recognised in the Western world for its health-giving, stress-relieving and creativity-enhancing benefits, as well as for spiritual attunement and to assist in the search for mystical experience.

Essentially, meditation is an altered state of consciousness in which a range of subtle physiological and mental changes help to bring about a feeling of serenity. Some industrial companies provide opportunity for personnel, particularly at the management level, to learn meditation so that the burdens of decision-making may be eased and new, creative ideas may come from a place of inner peace.

The practices by which the meditative state is achieved are often confused with the state itself. Alternate nostril breathing, breath counting, breath 'watching', the chanting of a mantra or the visualising of a rose are all means to an end.

In the meditative or ruminative state we become receptive, our perceptions are subject to delicate change and the less conscious reaches of our beings are more easily accessible. Thoughts, feelings, memories, images and symbols, which before may have been partially or wholly hidden, gently come to the surface to be recognised, owned and examined. (Further reading on meditation is recommended in the Bibliography.)

Guided Journeys

Guided journeys for self-exploration require, but also enable, a slightly altered state of consciousness in which the focus of our attention may be inwardly directed. Progressively they help us to become more familiar with 'what is inside' – or what is often termed the 'inner landscape' (see my book *A Question of Guidance*).

Through guided journeying, not only is information from within brought to the surface, but self-healing and enhancement of spiritual consciousness can become more personally directed or controlled. There is a time and tide, a rhythm or cycle in all things, but when the tide is right we need to use it as skilled surf-riders, rather than as flotsam and jetsam to be taken only where the wave wills.

As you travel from the source to the sea, each stage of the journey helps to lead you a little more deeply into yourself in order to 'clear' psychological material and reveal the next steps on your spiritual path. For this reason it is important to try to follow the journeys in sequence, unless you are already confident in this field or are working with an experienced therapist or outer world guide.

Journeying Safely

'Safety factors' are built into each journey and into the method of journeying. Relaxing and aligning your physical body helps to balance your chakras and subtle energies. Though it may sometimes seem repetitive, beginning in the meadow means that there is a safe place at the edge of normal waking consciousness and the inner worlds. Before you do any serious journeying, you reconnect with the meadow and activate all your inner senses. Before you return to the outer world you pass through the meadow, thus signalling to yourself that you are about to move from one area of your consciousness to another. If at any time you feel uncomfortable with anything in your inner world, then the meadow is there as the safe area of transition. There you can peacefully consider the inner happenings or rest awhile before you 'ease over' into the demands of the outer world.

Using the Heart Energy

In the induction to each inner journey, you are guided to open up your heart centre or chakra. The heart energy is a particularly safe and wise energy on which to travel. Activating it ensures that your experiences will be gentle and that you will only unveil those secrets of your psyche which you are able to deal with at any given time.

Gentle Revelation

Often you will be advised not to 'dig' into your past or memory, but to accept what comes. If you are enthusiastic about psychological and spiritual unfolding, it is tempting to test the boundaries and to force blocked memories to the surface. But the psyche is very wise and reveals its depths only in an environment of trust. When you remember something during an inner journey, even if it seems very familiar or mundane, your psyche will have a reason for giving you that memory at that time. If you respect this and work with what is given, then gradually and gently the deeper revelations too will emerge. Trauma and drama are not measurements of depth or speed of growth.

Symbols of Inner Protection

Whilst you are still in the meadow, or at other stages of your travelling, you may be asked to call to you, or make contact with, a talisman or amulet, an inner wise being or a power animal.

All of these are symbols for the power, strength or wisdom in your psyche. They help you to journey wisely and to be centred as you do so. If you are at a crossroads or have any kind of choice to make during a journey, these aspects of yourself will help in finding the right direction and making the right choice.

The talisman

A talisman in the inner world may be a reflection of something which also comforts you in the outer world. For some it is their childhood teddy bear or rocking horse, conveniently miniaturised or even animated for easier travel. For some the talisman may be more archetypal or classical – like a guiding star, a staff or lantern. It does not matter what form it takes, but it must have the ability to give you a special quality of safety and comfort whenever you touch it.

The amulet

An amulet may be similar to a talisman and has an allied function. You can have an amulet as well as, or instead of, a talisman. Whilst a talisman is something that has *become* special or meaningful to you, an amulet may in some way have been charged or blessed and is usually given to you by someone special or to mark a special moment. Like the talisman, the amulet may exist in the outer world as well as the inner. It is most likely to be a piece of jewellery, a precious stone or crystal, a beautiful bottle or casket, a jewelled knife, a sword or a chalice.

The talisman or amulet may remain constant and unchanging, or there may be special gifts for particular journeys. Most people who journey in the inner worlds end up with a collection of inner treasures!

The power animal

This concept has its roots in shamanistic lore. Animals can help us in the inner worlds. They protect us, guide us, mirror lessons for us and help us to stay in contact with our natural sense of what is right, wholesome and safe. With their aid we can see in the dark, swim under water whilst still breathing, fly and glide on air currents, walk through the fire and survive the swamp or the pit. The strong yet gentle power animals of our inner worlds may be very wild or fierce in the outer. When we cross the threshold to inner experience they become our friends, they may speak with us and they are our guides and protectors.

It is possible to meet animals in the inner worlds who are not friendly because they symbolise some inner conflict or imbalance, but the true power animal can always be trusted, will come when we call, track us when we stray, energise us when we are fatigued and help to heal us when we are ill. They are recognised by the light in their eyes and their joy at being found by us, or invited into the journey.

The Inner Wise Presence

In our good moments, when we make clear decisions or give wise non-judgemental advice to a friend, we know that there is access to a place of wisdom within. It has little to do with personal experience and is related to a knowledge of inner potential and the potential of humankind. In inner journeys this source of wisdom becomes personified. It may be a mythological being or animal, or it may simply be an atmosphere of sacredness and love. By learning in the inner worlds that we can call this being or presence to us at will, we can be led to deeper layers of self-understanding as well as being empowered to use its strength more often and consciously in outer life.

Some Comments on Symbolism

Symbolism is a big subject and suggestions for further reading are given in the Bibliography. As symbols come from your inner worlds, try to resist the temptation to over-analyse them. Their meaning will gradually unfold as you 'live' with them. If you want to read about your symbols, refer to the type of book which gives historical background and the meaning of the particular symbol in different cultures.

There are some symbol books which make categorical statements such as 'snake means transformation'. But you yourself hold the most important clues to interpreting your own symbols. What does this mean to you? If you have a very real fear of snakes and they come into your inner world or dreams, perhaps it will be some time before you can appreciate their transformative aspect. For you they may be asking that you work with that fear and identify it more.

The stage of exploring what a symbol means or has meant in your life is called the stage of association. Only when you have done this or got stuck should you turn to books or others for the next stage which is amplification. Gradually the symbol will live for you and reveal its layers of meaning.

Symbols are often confused with signs, and are used as signs in the world around us. The red cross on a white background signals that first aid is available. This is its meaning when used as a sign in the world of today. Yet this same cross is the cross of St George, who has association with dragons; it is the cross of the Crusaders and their religious wars; and it is a part of the Union Jack, the flag of the United Kingdom. In amplification as a symbol, the red cross encompasses all these possibilities and shades of meaning.

As an example of personal association to this same symbol, a client, who had seen a red cross in a dream, said: 'I went to a fancy dress party when I was six, dressed as a knight wearing a red cross. It was not a happy time of my life – my whole family was at a *crossroads*, and my mother was about to leave us with our father and an au pair I hated. My mother was always *cross* at that time – I saw her anger as bright *red* in colour. Perhaps my dream is telling me that I am even now wearing fancy dress in order to avoid the *crossroads*, anger and conflict I must face in my business affairs – and that I am no longer an insecure six-year-old about to be abandoned.'

When working further with my client's dream, he was able to accept that the message of the symbol was also about the crusading strength he possessed and the deeper resources he could draw on to resolve his present conflict.

A symbol is never simplistic in its meaning or significance. Because symbols are the means whereby the deeper reaches of our psyches speak to us, their wealth of meaning will only gradually unfold. Their presence in our consciousness is a gift. The symbol may help us to look at our inner difficulties; it may also reveal unsuspected strengths.

When a symbol appears it should be greeted with honour, reverence and excitement. Each one is an important stepping-stone to self-knowledge. Each one helps us to get beyond any mental façade created by the left brain and to have more contact with the insights and creativity of the right brain.

Keeping a Workbook

The fact that symbols only gradually reveal all their associations and amplificatons is an excellent reason for keeping a river of life workbook in which to record your progress through the exercises. A loose-leaf file has the advantage that extra pages can be slipped in at any point. There are some attractive binders in the shops now and it is important to have a pleasing setting for your recording. If you are very artistic you may prefer a large sketchbook to give you plenty of scope for drawings and illustrations. If you enjoy creative writing, then a book with a lovely cover may be inspirational. Only you can choose, but it is a choice worth thinking about. Rolled or folded paintings, drawings and diverse pieces of papers are not easy when you want to review the way your journey has unfolded.

The Psychological/ Spiritual Interface

Psychology is the study of perceptions, mind, behaviour, functioning, attitudes and driving forces within human beings, both individually and collectively. There are many branches of psychology, some of which are totally focused on human behaviour patterns and their modification.

Over the last sixty to seventy years there has been an increasing interest in transpersonal psychology, which lays its greatest emphasis on the drive within the individual to find meaning in life. It is a psychology based originally on the work of Jung, Assagioli, Frankl and Maslow.

Those of us most likely to take the transpersonal psychological journey are, in the words of Jung, 'discontent with being normal'. In recent years transpersonal psychologies have become linked with such phrases as 'human potential'. The transpersonal way is that which leads us to discover the best within ourselves and each other, and to come to creative terms with the conditioning and expectations of society and parents. As we discover who we really are, 'achievement' in the traditional outer sense – which often denies the feeling, intuitive and aesthetic sides of our nature – may be thrown aside in a major reconsideration of values, priorities and the quality of life.

Most transpersonal psychologies consider that there is a higher motivating force which enables us to bring a spiritual dimension into our living.

The word 'spiritual' can be very widely defined. It need have little to do with religion, faith or God. Maslow spoke of the 'meta needs' of humankind, and of how their pursuit and presence aids the journey to individual and collective potential. These meta needs include justice, beauty, peace, unconditional love, higher education and the fine arts. Frankl, studying the factors which had enabled people to survive their terrible imprisonment in concentration camps, spoke of the drive to find 'symbolic meaning' in life.

The new age movement has a tendency to confuse transpersonal psychologies with esoteric spiritual pursuits. There is, of course, a place where the disciplines meet, but they are complementary fields – the one does not automatically include the other. It is unwise to pursue esoteric paths such as 'channelling', healing, chakra development, assiduous forms of meditation, shamanism, rebirthing and past life exploration without also seeking sound psychological self-understanding.

Spirituality is not a state of over-fragility in which materialism, sensuality and the body are rejected. Sensitivity is not a condition which means that the demands of everyday living cannot be tolerated. True spiritual growth and the development of sensitivity enable us to function fully and successfully in the world whilst questioning all value systems and seeking, if not actively campaigning for, a universal quality of life as the right of every human being in incarnation.

Some Common Questions and Fears about Inner Journeying

Is there any danger that I could get lost, go too deep or feel out of control?

Inner journeying is a sound and safe way of gaining self-knowledge. The psyche has a wisdom within it and will rarely confront the ego with material which is too deep or over-painful. Symbols help us to go deeper but because of their nature their meaning unfolds gradually, in layers, at a speed which is paced for each individual. This is another reason why it is wise to 'live' with the symbol rather than to be in too much of a rush to get it 'interpreted'.

Research has confirmed that in inner journeys or meditative states you cannot get lost never to return. Without the structure of a guided journey it is possible to get absorbed and lose track of time, but eventually you would return, as from sleep, without ill-effect. This common fear can be overcome by following only guided journeys. Record those in this book onto a cassette, leaving the necessary spaces in the recording for the inner explorations you are guided to make. In this way you do not have to worry about remembering everything and you can relax without feeling the need to watch the clock.

You may enjoy journeying alone, but if you find it easier to have company invite a partner, friend or small group of friends to become co-travellers. Sharing the experiences of the journey can be exciting and reassuring.

If you are very anxious or stressed and are new to this sort of work, find some workshops where guided imagery is practised before you start to work alone.

If at any time you have questions about your growth process or need advice, a trained transpersonal counsellor or psychosynthesis guide can be consulted.

If you are receiving treatment for a psychological or mental condition, always consult your advisers before undertaking inner work of this kind, especially if you intend to work alone.

I have difficulty in visualisation. I don't seem to 'see' as others do. I feel that I create mentally everything that happens and that therefore it is not valid. Perhaps this way is not the right one for me?

Without doubt, for some people the inner world is a landscape with a complete life of its own, For others the imagination plays an active part in creating what is experienced. Guided journeys aid the imagination to set the scene until the experience gains its own momentum.

Where, as with the question above, the process is more pedestrian and mental, it is still valid. We are all more able to visualise than we may think, but even if it seems that you are 'making up a story', take into consideration the many thousands of permutations you *could* use.

Your psyche, albeit through the mental process, will lead you to a combination which has meaning for you at this time, and this should be respected.

Emphasis on the intuition and the current eagerness for visual, right brain experience has tended to devalue the thinking or mental function. A balance is necessary, but those who think things out rather than 'intuiting' them should not be deterred from inner explorations. Every aspect of us is part of the river of life.

Guided Journey to Contact Your Inner Wise Presence

Make sure that you will be undisturbed and provide yourself with a rug or blanket for warmth, then find a relaxed but balanced and supported position for your body . . . Close your eyes . . . be aware of the rhythm of your breathing . . . and bring that rhythm into your heart centre, thus activating the heart energy on which to travel into your inner landscape . . . Find yourself in the meadow . . . activate all your inner senses so that you see the objects and colours . . . hear the sounds . . . touch the textures . . . smell the fragrances . . . and taste the tastes.

Recall your previous journey to the River of Life and be aware of how to reach the river from your meadow . . . Be aware of your inner landscape around and beyond the river . . . In the first journey you intuitively called to you any animal, talisman, amulet or object which would be useful on your journey . . . ask for any of these to be present with you now . . . Know that somewhere in this landscape your inner wise presence dwells . . . You can either journey to that dwelling-place, for a part of you knows well how to find the pathway . . . or you can call the wise presence towards you now, in the meadow . . .

At your journey's goal or when you call, you may
experience an atmosphere of wise understanding, see
colours, hear a beautiful sound, smell a special fragrance
or meet with a being . . . as you either experience this
presence or see your inner wise being, ask for a blessing
on the journeys you intend to make. You may receive a
special gift or talisman for use with these particular
journeys, be given a key-word or feel a lightening of
your heart and a knowledge that you are guided and
protected . . . If you receive or experience none of these,
then know that there will be other opportunities during
the journeys to meet with your wise presence, and that
this initial invocation has nevertheless been important in
paving the way . . .

Spend up to ten minutes enjoying your inner wise
presence and then, if you have journeyed beyond it,
return to your meadow . . . to the rhythm of your
breathing in your heart centre . . . to your awareness of
your body, your contact with the ground and your
normal surroundings . . . Imagine that there is a cloak of
light with a hood right around you . . . Take your
pencils, pens and crayons and record your journey.

3

The Source of the River

Nature's handmaid art,
Makes mighty things from small beginnings grow.

JOHN DRYDEN

Birth ... The meaning and purpose of incarnation ... Embodiment ... Aspects of the greater self ... Are there laws of manifestation governing physical as well as spiritual life? ... Do we form our own world? ... Can we release ourselves from past conditioning?

Birth

Although it is possible to remember being born, it is unlikely for the memory to be recovered spontaneously. Deep psychotherapy, forms of hypnosis, abreaction through medication or experiences during drug use are the usual triggers which unveil this particular recall.

Most of us are told many things about the circumstances of our birth: the rush to the hospital, the delayed arrival of the midwife, the baby that comes a month too early ... or a month too late ... the excitement, the joys and the fears are the stuff of family history and help to put us in touch with our roots. These days the family home video library may contain full, graphic tapes of every stage of our bodily journey into the world. With so much information available and more openness and sharing in the whole process of giving birth, the younger generation may have a greater conscious appreciation of, and connection to, their physical origins. Finding our footing in incarnation in this way is important, but it is also a spiritual task and we must be careful not to lose contact with the higher mysteries of existence.

When a child asks: 'Where do babies come from?' parents often begin the daunting task of teaching 'the facts of life'. The child may be very astonished at being answered on this level. After wide experience of teaching young children I am convinced that the interest behind many of their questions, particularly about the workings of the universe, is metaphysical. Answers which are only factually or scientifically based not only beg the spiritual implications but may offer too much detail too soon and make learning seem a dense and over-demanding task. Turning the question back to the child helps to clarify what sort of response is being sought. Their asking may arise from wanting to share an inner wonderment. Their own thoughts about matters of origin often have an inspirational quality.

On responding 'Where do *you* think they come from?' to the question above, I have received these answers from four- and five-year-olds: 'From light made by the stars', 'From God', 'From the rainbow', 'From the angels', 'From love', 'From heaven.' Such children are, in Wordsworth's phrase, 'trailing clouds of glory'. They are in touch with the wonder of life. They do not need answers so much as affirmation.

The ones who giggle and answer: 'Out of the nurse's bag', 'Out of Mummy's tummy', or 'You buy them at the hospital' have partial or unsatisfactory factual information and may indeed be ready to know more on this level. They may also be expressing a dissatisfaction that something as powerful as birth has been reduced to the mundane.

As adults seeking spiritual answers to the questions: 'Where do I come from and what is my purpose?' we must also be careful not to get overwhelmed by intricate, esoteric explanations. Having a working hypothesis increases our sense of meaning. Grappling too hard with dogma or formulae impoverishes our sense of wonder and separates us from the inner 'golden child' (see page 60) who still sees, in Wordsworth's words:

> *The earth, and every common sight . . .*
> *Apparelled in celestial light*
> *The glory and the freshness of a dream.*

Although in this chapter Gildas gives some formulated answers, the inner journey to the source on page 45 is intended to restore a sense of reverence, along with other insights about your particular experience.

The Meaning and Purpose of Incarnation

Without spiritual belief (and spiritual is not necessarily religious), life and its purpose must remain a conundrum.

Dogmatic belief systems give ethical codes, and usually some promise of eternal life. They postulate an eventual state of bliss as a reward for those who successfully complete the path. Various models of hell or purgatory are also described as the fate or interim experience of those who fail to follow the rules or who backslide. Fundamentalist interpretations of spiritual and religious teachings often lead into the very complexities which they originally set out to avoid. 'God is Love' does not sit easily alongside 'The Lord thy God is a jealous God'. Systems which proclaim an almighty, all-controlling, often anthropomorphic divinity flounder when it comes to the problem of suffering.

Nevertheless, ancient beliefs often contain powerful elements of superstition. A plethora of gods and goddesses may be more effective in demonstrating that the power behind the universe is many-faceted and beyond finite comprehension.

It might seem logical that religions could agree to differ or to accept that each of them covers a facet of the greater truth. Instead they deny their basic tenets by resorting to war, torture, coercion and extortion, and leave the would-be believer bewildered.

Too many gods lead to confusion. Too much intellectual discussion of dogma leads to 'noise' and away from reverence. Yet extreme silence does not satisfy the mind. Science and religion have taken divergent pathways towards an understanding of the universe and its guiding principles.

Today there are signs that scientists and mystics may reach a complementary understanding. Pictures of the energy patterns within order as well as within chaos, the discovery of sub-atomic particles and their behaviour, and the proof that what is observed is affected by the observer render the boundary between physics and metaphysics less clearly defined.

Our spiritual well-being is helped by 'symbolic understanding'. Viktor Frankl's study of survivors from concentration camps showed that a belief in there being a wider, symbolic meaning to personal suffering was a significant survival factor. We need a return to the myth; not in the primitive sense where the myth has power over us, but in the more sophisticated sense in which we can use the myth and the archetype to stretch our understanding of the great and infinite mysteries in which we partake.

Having a belief in the common purpose of life helps us to find a sense of individual purpose. The search for the latter is often frustrating and painful. We live in a 'doing'-orientated society. When individuals ask Gildas about their purpose, he will often answer that the purpose of each human incarnation is growth, which needs to be balanced in 'being' as well as in activity. He also often gives key-words to describe the overall purpose he may see 'coming in' from the higher self. These are almost invariably linked to the archetypes of higher qualities.

He describes us, for example, as being under the umbrella of the healer, the writer, the communicator, the leader, the teacher, the artist, the architect, the creator of beauty and harmony, the seer, the builder the bridge-builder, the priest/healer, the server, the pioneer, the mountaineer, the navigator, the mother, the father – or perhaps a combination of two or more of these.

Having knowledge of our 'overlighting archetype' does not necessarily infer that we have to go out into the world and become it, or take it on as an active outer identity. It means, rather, that we can invest the 'style' of that key-word into whatever we happen to be doing. Once given this insight, we may be inspired to make big changes in our lives. This is not always easy or possible, particularly in the short term, but we may be able to 'lift' the very situation which is frustrating us by dealing with it from a different perspective. When I was frustrated with teaching young children but, being a single parent, needed to continue, at a crisis point I found the strength to go on by identifying more with 'the healer' and by focusing on every opportunity to become more involved in the pastoral side of teaching.

Embodiment

This word might be seen as a synonym for 'incarnation'. Here, the latter is used to describe the whole process of coming into life on earth as a human being, whilst 'embodiment' refers more specifically to our bodies and that which lives within them. There are things about our bodies which we cannot change. Much of what we are able or unable to do in life is dependent upon our genetic inheritance and the physical and mental capacities with which we are endowed.

Yet what do we embody other than physical and mental attributes and abilities? Each one of us within the genetic family, even perhaps born as an identical twin, is unique not just in body but also in other less tangible ways. Students of human behaviour constantly debate, and endeavour to isolate, the factors which create the difference. Mind and spirit are numinous. Even now that it is possible to study the brain more minutely, the mind cannot be scientifically located. Spirit is even more difficult. Most would argue that mind and intellect are related; but the force of individuality which is in each one of us, and which we recognise in each other, is resistant to scientific study.

Aspects of the Greater Self

In esoteric study we encounter further difficulties in defining or separating that which is spirit and that which is soul. In such areas we are largely dependent on what we feel, but most arcane writers and teachers accept that there is a difference between the two. These are also seen as the essence which is eternal. Their imprint makes us individual and unique, and their subtle substance is everlasting.

Most spiritual teachings imply that a part of the essences which are soul and spirit does not become embodied, but watches over us from a more subtle plane. Some alchemical teachings proclaim the spirit to be yang – direct, focused, active and clear, whilst the soul is yin – diffuse, receptive, reflective, absorbent and containing. The spirit is likened to a flame and the soul to a chalice. When the flame burns brightly within the containing chalice, then the alchemical marriage is achieved and the golden child is born.

Incarnation and embodiment cause a separation of soul and spirit which is necessary to the learning and refining process. The spirit plunges into matter and darkness (incarnation). The soul absorbs, reflects and records the experience. As the incarnate being becomes conscious of the in-dwelling spirit, so trust in a meaning and pattern to life is born. Incarnate being, in-dwelling spirit and soul/higher self-function as one, in total awareness. In alchemical terms, the dross burns away and the base metal turns into gold.

Spiritual alchemists, though often believing in reincarnation, sought the secret of completing this union within one lifetime. Other esoteric teachings describe a similar process of refinement, but see the journey as an evolutionary one taking many lifetimes. Most teachings agree that the task is collective as well as individual.

In Greek the word for spirit is 'pneuma', which is also the word for breath. When speaking of spirit, words such as 'aspiration' and 'inspiration' are often used. Thus the spirit is that which breathes us and animates our spiritual life-force.

Are there laws of manifestation governing physical as well as spiritual life?

Spiritually we manifest the life opportunities and experiences for which we are ready and which will temper our spiritual strength. We may ask what exactly 'spiritual strength' means. Its ingredients are integrity or congruence, vision, non-attachment, moral courage or fibre, non-judgementalism and unconditional love. Integrity or congruence is the quality which enables all our actions to be in harmony. The spiritually strong person radiates a sense of wholeness. Vision is the ability to see the wider picture. Non-attachment is neither emotional coldness nor a denigration and denial of physical and material comforts. It is a state of non-possessiveness in material life and relationships. Moral courage or fibre is similar to integrity. It involves an inner rather than an outer ethical code, and the ability to stand by it even at great personal cost. Non-judgementalism does not mean *lack* of judgement or discernment but the ability to combine these with compassion. Unconditional love is not an 'anything goes' attitude but the ability to love the human/divine spark in everyone without arrogance or patronage.

The goal of any incarnation might be summarised as 'the gaining and tempering of spiritual strength'. If we believe that life is a school, then the laws of spiritual manifestation are linked to the path of spiritual growth. In ancient times there was set training for those who sought initiation. Newborn children would even be surveyed by a seer to see if they were ready for conscious spiritual training. If so, they would go to live in the temple from a very early age. The community depended upon priests and priestesses for counselling, guidance, healing, dream interpretation and the performance of rituals which made the crops grow, ushered in the seasons, celebrated the harvest, governed weather and fertility, appeased the evil forces and enabled communion with the divine, or a sense of the mystical.

Today it is still possible to find a spiritual teacher or guru. We can, if we wish, become devotees or enter an enclosed spiritual order. But the community no longer depends explicitly upon such callings. Instead we have the welfare state, a concept based on high and even spiritual idealism which has become politically trammelled.

We live, therefore, in an age of self-initiation. We find and govern our own spiritual paths. We are spiritually eclectic. Many ways are open and available. Without a specific teacher or spiritual director the way can be lonely.

Yet there are 'laws' of spiritual manifestation and the well-known directives can be our signposts. 'Seek and ye shall find'; 'When one door closes another opens'; 'When the pupil is ready the teacher is there'; 'Knock and it shall be opened unto you'; 'Be still and know'; 'Surrender your ego and find your soul'. And many more.

'When the pupil is ready, the teacher is there' is too often interpreted as promising a flesh-and-blood teacher, who may appear, but we need also to recognise life itself as our teacher. When we are strong enough to accept the lesson, it will be presented to us.

'Surrender your ego and find your soul' has been badly and even dangerously interpreted as meaning that we should be 'egoless', which is actually a form of schizophrenia or psychosis. We cannot surrender something which we do not have, and the ego needs to be carefully nurtured if the spiritual path is to be effective.

Eventually the well-tempered ego will surrender gracefully to the knowledge and directives of the greater self and be a finely tuned instrument for the higher will. Individuals who have honoured this process make a clear contribution to human endeavour. Those who ignore it may be burned by the flame or mistake the path of egocentricity and self-interest for the journey of the soul.

There is a spiritual 'rule of three'. Ask or knock three times, and the lesson or spiritual gift manifests. Before you do so, be *very* clear what you are asking for and study well all possible implications and ramifications.

Do we form our own world?

Do such laws of manifestation apply also to material life? To some extent they do. We can live magically. This does not necessarily mean that we can conjure up all the material possessions and wealth we might crave. We have to make a clear definition between 'needs' and 'wants'. For some, material needs may be very basic, while for others they are genuinely more elaborate. If the spiritual law of non-attachment is being learned, it will be easier to find a balance and to remember that denying the material does not necessarily accelerate the spiritual, especially in the world to which we have to adjust today.

In order to help material life flow for us, we need an awareness of abundance without prodigality or greed. Prodigality pollutes. Greed and stockpiling prevent us recognising that there are more than enough resources of all kinds for the world population. What is true for the collective is true for the individual.

Endeavouring to welcome abundance into our lives is an enlightening but daunting task. It challenges all our basic insecurities and negative belief systems. Abundance is a flow. If our insecurities make us into hoarders; if we have poor self-esteem and feel we are 'not good enough'; if we need permission to have fun or comfort; or if we have a belief in a mean-minded, vengeful and jealous God; in all these situations we block the flow. Those who believe that they should sell everything and give to the poor might reflect that so doing only creates another poor person. The problem of poverty is not so easily solvable, but if we are in the flow of abundance we are freer to notice the needs of others and to act abundantly towards them.

We *do* create our own world, mainly by our attitudes, belief systems and angle of perception. Believing and knowing that we are in the right place at the right time can help us adjust to the lessons the material world brings us. It can also enable the increase of 'positive synchronicity' in our lives, so that we make the right connections, attract the right opportunities and facilitate the task of our guides and guardian angels. 'I am and will be in the right place at the right time' is a good affirmation when learning to live magically and to form our own world more positively.

Can we release ourselves from past conditioning?

Conditioning comes from society and from parents and teachers who have themselves been conditioned by that society. Getting clear of it is full of complexities and involves clear insight and the making of choices. The pioneers and true reformers will not only want to free themselves from conditioned structures but will want to change some of the collectively held paradigms. Yet each individual who struggles for freedom also influences the whole.

Successful release from conditioning means facing the power of the collective paradigm as well as that of the explicit and implicit teachings, permissions and taboos received from parents. The journey into having more clarity about these and their effects upon us is part of the work entailed in undertaking the voyage along the River of Life as set out in this book. When we recognise the source of our inner messages we put ourselves in a position of choice and help ourselves to build a more solid, true identity. Which messages will we accept or own? Which will we reject? Where we disagree, what will we do about changing our attitudes? What will we put in the place of that which we reject? A personal ethical code, rather than an imposed moral one, is an essential foundation to growth.

To deny all conformity would be to throw out the baby with the bath water. To question it nourishes our identity. Release from conditioning brings a sense of freedom. It is a lifelong task that needs constant revision, like clearing out the store cupboard, but it is well worth the effort.

I now hand the rest of this chapter over to Gildas.

GILDAS

Greetings! I welcome the opportunity to be able to communicate via the pages of this book. At this point I should like to add some thoughts about the meaning and purpose of life.

It is inevitable that, whilst incarnate, your main focus will be on the immediate and present lifespan. Your models of progression are linear and hierarchical. You are bound by the time dimension. Even if you believe in reincarnation it is difficult for you to see the life in which you are, at any given moment, as part of a much broader continuum.

Linear and hierarchical modelling lead easily to the assumption that cause and effect have a simple progression. Themes around 'growth' or 'goodness' and theories of being required to reach some standard of perfection lie behind most conjecture about the meaning and purpose of life.

From such a basis it is natural to believe in a system of punishment and reward. You make an action. It brings results. According to those results you receive either punishment or reward. The more rewards you receive the higher up the scale of goodness you go – unless you learn from your punishments you will continue to be oppressed or ostracised. Non-conformity is automatically a punishable offence. This is a very primitive system and one which is hardly founded on love.

Yet this is the system which has been projected on to divine intelligence! These are the thoughts which cause gross misunderstanding and misinterpretation of the karmic laws of cause and effect.

You come from the divine. Your basic essence is a divine spark. Separating from the source and journeying back again could be a wonderful process. Your separation from the source was not caused by a fall from grace. The return journey is not an eternal punishment or curse vented by a jealous god because the first woman dared to eat of the fruit of the tree of knowledge and seduce her mate into doing likewise. Rather, it is a sacred mystery which ensures that nothing in the universe becomes static and that there can be a continual communion and interaction between creator and created.

In order to understand this mystery you must strive to slough off all old, negative conditioning about the nature of the human journey. You must also strive to remove all anthropomorphic and finite limitations from your image of the divine. Broaden and temper your vision of the power behind the universe by contemplating the concept of unconditional love.

It has been said that human beings are created in the divine image. I would reflect that more often the divine is conceptualised in the image of the human – and not the highest-principled human at that. This is a thought form or conditioning which must be overcome if the personal and collective spiritual journey to harmonious life is to succeed.

Thus the purpose of life may be seen as a blessed, rather than a cursed, journey from the source and back again. The human spark has not been banished from paradise, but has entered an agreement to make the journey of knowledge in order that more of the many facets of divine truth may be experienced and understood; indeed, in order that the divine may become more conscious of itself.

The journey of consiousness can be painful, dangerous and full of pitfalls as, in your present age, you are only too aware. Yet your very awareness of the dangers is a sign that the hard part of that journey is almost over. Once you understand the spectrum of human possibility with all its horrors and its glories, then you will be in a position of true choice and can set aside those aspects of human nature and existence which are unlovely, non-sacred and negatively destructive. The energy which goes into such manifestations may be reclaimed so that a state of health, harmony and peace may exist on earth as a golden age dawns.

Facing choice means facing responsibility. Sometimes it may be easier to believe that your growth is in the hands of an authority. When you do wrong you will be punished, when you do right you will be rewarded. It is far more challenging to realise that the system is one of self-limitation and self-reward. In the area to which you travel between lives you make an intensive review of the life which has just been lived, seeing it from a position of broader perspective, so that the many ripples of cause and effect can be most fully perceived and understood. From here, decisions about the next life which will be undertaken and the conditions, limitations, tasks and lessons for that life can be made.

These decisions are not necessarily based on the concept of 'growing good' – but on gaining experience. If the jewel of truth has many facets, then each of those facets may represent a lifetime's exploration. Thus the total jewel represents the total journey of evolution. The limitations which you take on in any given lifetime are not the yoke of punishment but boundaries to help you become more conscious of where your task lies. The gifts and potentials which you bring with you enable you to balance, through service, those things which may have gone awry in a previous lifetime. They are not only your gifts to yourself but your gifts to humanity and the human condition. The limitations which you bring help to show you where your strengths lie, give you definition, mark the path more clearly and help you to discover who you really are. Eventually the spiritual path will reveal to you that your limitations can become your greatest assets.

Your fears in life often relate to the possibility of making wrong choices. There is little opportunity for this to happen within the broad confines laid down by the higher self. All choice leads to experience. A spectrum of experience is the ultimate goal. The higher self makes an overall selection of possibilities for each lifetime. These include the choice of gender, parents, culture, body and specific gifts or functional limitations. In this way all choice for the incarnated personality is circumscribed, though that circumscription may be wide. Within its circle the only wrong choices are over-passivity – which amounts to a rejection of all life and evolutionary opportunities – and deliberately following a path of greed, corruption, tyranny or destructive intent towards one's fellow human beings.

Life is meant to be joyful and related to beauty and love. It is not a prison sentence but an opportunity to enjoy potential. The over-lighting purpose of life is to work towards a state of co-creativity with the divine. The promised Golden Age is not for powerless and unconscious innocents wandering in the Garden of Eden but for empowered, fully conscious beings, delighting – and taking full part in – the unfolding art and miracle of creation.

Exercises Relating to this Chapter

Guided Journey to the Source of the River

Sit or lie in a comfortable but symmetrically balanced
position. Make sure that you will be undisturbed, and
that you have a blanket for warmth and crayons and
paper on hand for any recording you wish to do.

Be aware of the rhythm of your breathing . . .
gradually bring that rhythm into your heart centre or
chakra, and travel, on the heart energy, into your inner
landscape . . . find yourself in the meadow . . . ask for
your inner wise presence to accompany you or to bless
this journey, and make sure that you have any talisman
or amulet you wish to take . . . There is a pathway
which leads from where you now stand to the River of
Life . . . Follow the path, and when you are standing
beside the river, activate all your inner senses . . . see the
objects and colours . . . hear the sounds . . . smell the
fragrances . . . touch the textures . . . and taste the tastes
. . . Be aware of the flow of the river . . . In one direction
it flows to the sea . . . in the other lies its source . . . Near
the place where you have joined the river there is a
landing-stage, with a river boat moored there, facing the
direction of the source . . . The guardians of the boat are
the shining presence of your inner wise being together
with your guardian angel (see page 80) . . . Approach
the boat and look at it . . . What kind of boat is it? . . .
How is it powered? . . . Who, of those present, will steer
it/sail it/ row it/drive it? . . .

When you wish to board the boat, you will be
welcomed and helped aboard by your personified inner
wise being and your guardian angel . . . When you are
ready to move off, it is you who will give the command

. . . Make sure that you are in a good position, from
where you can view the river ahead as you proceed
towards its source . . .

As you go, you will be aware that you are journeying
back through your life before its present point . . . You
may be aware of islands, backwaters, weedy patches,
muddy pools, areas of very clear water, whirlpools,
rapids, turgid waters, sheltered places, sunny regions,
dangerous currents and the many other reaches which
form part of a mighty river . . . You may hear a child's
voice or glimpse children playing on the banks . . . As
you journey, this is a time to observe – not to engage
with what you see, but to make a mental note of it for
future reference . . .

Now your goal is the source . . . As you come near to
that place it may become impossible for the river boat to
continue . . . the source may be in the mountains,
springing from the rocks themselves . . . It may well up
from grassy lands . . . It may begin as a trickle or as a
mighty waterfall . . . When the time comes for you to
leave the boat and walk, your guardians will accompany
you, but as you reach the source they will stand aside
and allow you to approach this point with reverence . . .

Not only water but also light comes from this source
. . . and as you come to it, you are bathed in light and
healing . . . Walk or climb to just beyond or above the
source, if you can, but in any case turn so that you face
in the direction of the flow . . . looking out on the river
of your life as it makes its journey to the sea . . . If you
are at a vantage point you may be able to see the whole
of the river's course . . . Or you may see just a portion of
it . . . As you stand, facing the direction of the flow, your
wise being and your angel will come to stand a little
behind or to each side of you . . . The light and flow in
which you are bathed is the essence of your life . . . your

life-force . . . life-spark . . . life-flow . . . You will become aware of a strong beam of coloured light which you recognise as the light of your higher self . . . You may sense other presences or essences here with you . . . perhaps the essence of your parents, grandparents, life partner(s), siblings, dear friends or teachers who are a part of your life's voyage . . .

Bathed in light, contemplate this place and your awareness of any presences . . . Take up to fifteen minutes for this contemplation, asking for any understanding of your life choices and purposes, any overview of your life's voyage, any inspiration from, or communion with, your higher self . . .

When you are ready, your wise presence and your guardian angel will lead you back to the boat and together you will return to the landing-stage from which this voyage began . . . From there you will return to the meadow . . . to the breath in your heart centre . . . to an awareness of your everyday surroundings . . .

Take time to record your journey and visualise a cloak of light with a hood of light right around you before you return to your normal tasks.

Reflection on Your Journey

As you record and reflect on your journey there are some points which may lead to further exploration and deeper insights.

What sort of boat did you find at the landing-stage?
These vary greatly from Viking ships complete with figurehead, gracefully rigged sailing ships, paddle steamers, rafts and coracles to more modern motorised vessels, launches, rowing boats, sailing boats and canoes.

Treat your boat as a symbol. Reflect on its significance

and associations for you. Is your approach to your
journey that of a spiritual warrior? Are you more of an
explorer? Are your tools for the journey simple or
sophisticated? Are you happy to be close to the river and
more directly in touch with it (rowing boats, coracles,
canoes, simple sailing boats)? Or do you require the
'distancing' and protection which a larger boat would give?

Who was guiding your boat – who was helping to power it?
If your wise presence and your guardian angel were
fully in charge, reflect on whether you are leaving it all
to them or whether you have already made a graceful
but empowered surrender to their guidance.

If you were doing most of the work alone, reflect on
whether you feel the spirtual journey should be gruelling
and full of graft, or whether, perhaps, you are too
independent and therefore need to work on issues around
cooperative trust.

Who was at your source and how did you experience them?
By journeying to the source it is possible to get a fresh
viewpoint on the roles of the significant people in your
life and your relationships with them. Reflect on why
you chose your parents and the lessons and mirroring
given by and exchanged with the people who are most
important in your life.

If you are a parent yourself, were your children at the
source? Why did they select you as 'their' parent? Why
did you attract them to be your children? What lessons/
gifts do you carry for each other?

The landscape as you journeyed
The river of childhood is the theme of the next guided
journey (see page 68) but, as you reflect on what you
passed in this journey, become aware of areas you would

like to explore more thoroughly, as a preparation for the next stage.

The light stream from your higher self
If this had a particular colour, first reflect on what that colour means to you and then turn to the Glossary for further colour information.

Spiritual and Material Manifestation – Forming Your Own World

Ask yourself what you need from your spiritual path. Are there any life changes, choices or commitments you need to make in order to help your needs to manifest?

Ask yourself the same questions about your material life and/or career.

What seem to be your main blockages to change or to the achievement of your aims?

Do your aims or your attitudes need revision?

Are you living out someone else's expectations of you?

Are you seeking some kind of 'permission' in order to go forward?

(You will get more help with insight into some of these questions as the voyage continues.)

Case History: The Source of the River

Helena was depressed and dissatisfied with her life and relationships. After marrying at eighteen, and with two children having arrived in quick succession, she now felt trapped. With a teenage son and daughter, herself only in her early thirties, she was unsure of her true identity. Her husband was a good provider but worked long hours, and their communication had lost all stimulus. The children had entered a particularly demanding phase, both emotionally and materially. Helena felt un-supported in her attempts to help them with the impor-tant transition into adulthood whilst maintaining enough boundaries to keep life running smoothly.

In the early days, she and her husband, Nick, had been carried along on a romantic 'high', which was even increased by the speedy arrival of the babies. Nick was only four years older than Helena, but an attractive wife and two perfect babies had spurred him on to early successes in his business career. They seemed the perfect couple. The children were not seriously rebellious, there were no real material worries. Outwardly their marriage seemed to be standing the tests of time.

Helena had come to feel they were living out a stereo-type. Beneath her depression and dissatisfaction she was in an identity crisis. She was a wife, a good mother, half of a perfect couple, a good housewife and home-manager with a lovely home. Yet sometimes she felt the only space which was truly hers was her side of the double bed.

The early marriage, straight from school, meant that she had no skills which might be viable outside the home, no activities which were separate from being Nick's wife and the children's mother. She was seriously questioning the meaning of life and wanting to know her core self.

She picked up one of my books in her local library and decided to come to a workshop in which the journey to the source of the river was the main focus of the day. At her source she recognised the essence of Nick, of her parents and of her two children. Seeing them there, she began to explore the possibility of a 'spiritual growth con-tract' between these key figures and herself.

Helena was the only child of rather intellectual parents who worked as researchers and translators. Her mother and father had a very absorbing relationship from which

Helena had felt excluded. When she and Nick had announced their engagement whilst Helena was still at school she had feared there might be some parental opposition. Instead, it had seemed to her that there was some sense of relief. Her father had rather vaguely intimated that he had been prepared to support her through university or other training. Her mother said: 'You must do what makes you happy', helped to organise a lovely wedding, waved goodbye as they left on honeymoon and returned to her books. As grandparents they liked to see the children occasionally and were generous but dutiful about Christmas and birthday presents.

They had been caring parents in their own way, but emotional engagement beyond their own rather symbiotic relationship was difficult for them.

Seeing them at the source, Helena realised that they had given her a self-sufficiency which she valued. They had also given her a good mind and an appreciation of literature and mythology which she had not yet used to the full.

Meeting Nick's essence, Helena awakened anew to the strong underlying spiritual bond between them. The stresses of family life had made it seem as though they were on divergent paths. She had feared that the early fires and passions of their love had burned out and ebbed away, leaving only ashes. Now she realised that though, at present, they were mirroring some difficult lessons for each other, the vital spark between them was still warm.

Seeing the essence of her children at the source, Helena recognised that they, too, were spiritual companions. She felt honoured that she and Nick had been chosen as their parents. In a quick review of their life together she was able to relive the joy of shared parenthood and the progressive bonding with the children. She realised that the current difficult phase would pass and that, in its own way, it was an exciting one. Beth and Barney were preparing for independence and adulthood, not just rejecting all that she and Nick had given them.

These insights at the source were no magical formula, and Helena's life did not change overnight; but she renewed her vision and determination. She saw that she needed interests of her own. She found the workshops supportive in expanding her spiritual search. Quite soon she also decided to be trained by, and work for, a voluntary counselling organisation. She joined a creative writing class and rediscovered a flair she had forgotten.

Nick responded very quickly as Helena began to take interest in herself and life once more. He suggested they should take a holiday alone. They put effort into bringing the zest back into their marriage and began to enjoy anew all the benefits of life which they had worked so hard to achieve. Today, Helena tends to agree with the comment 'You are the perfect couple', rather than finding it irksome.

4

The River of Childhood

Childhood is not from birth to a certain age and at
  a certain age
The child is grown, and puts away childish things,
Childhood is the kingdom where nobody dies.
Nobody that matters, that is.

EDNA ST VINCENT MILLAY

*The conditioned well self . . . The true well self . . . The
inner child . . . The golden child . . . Obedience . . . Forgiveness . . . Karma . . . Cutting 'the ties which bind' . . . The
remedial zone of the astral plane . . .*

The Conditioned Well Self

Conditioning was referred to briefly in Chapter 3. It
plays a large role in our lives and is often the channel
by which we lose sight of the true self, or seed.

When gardening, we take care to put our plants into
the amalgam of soil and environment which we know will
encourage them to grow as well as possible. We note
whether our nurslings like to be reasonably dry or well
watered; we transplant them if they are too crowded or do
not have enough light and shade to enable them to grow.

If we grow seeds or plants which have lost their labels,
we watch, with interest, their reactions to the environment
in which we have put them and endeavour to discover

what suits them best. When they fruit or flower we accept what they produce, knowing that the plant contains a blueprint and that we cannot influence poppy seeds to become cucumbers or force plants of unknown origin to produce what we *will* them to produce.

Our society is both complex and stereotyped. In the symbolic, if not the absolute, sense children are often force-fed, starved of stimulus, strenuously moulded, denied choice and individuality or required to fit 'convenient' structures. We lay a dangerous emphasis on the 'norm', which can lead to non-recognition of outstanding creativity or genius.

The Search for Approval

Our longing for approval is one of the strongest of human urges. It places a strong weapon in the hands of those who wield authority. All can be well if that authority is tempered with wisdom and love. But much can go wrong if love is possessive or when there is a chain reaction of conformity based on fear, when the requirements of society have not been questioned or when a sense of frustration causes tunnel vision.

The child's longing for approval invests parents or teachers with the authority to fashion the basic mores and social graces which enable family and community life to run smoothly. This is necessary. Yet that same longing for approval can also create a power which is subtly corrupt.

The psychologist Carl Rogers insisted that a major requirement for successful psychotherapy is that the therapist should be able to maintain 'unconditional positive regard' for the client. This does not mean that the client is not to be helped to behavioural changes or discernment, but that the basic human essence must be seen and valued before healthy growth can take place. Many parents would do well to remember that axiom.

So often the child gets the message of *conditional* love or regard. Do what *we* want you to do, become what *we* want you to become, be the success *I* never was, do not question *our* values, make us proud of you on *our* terms and all will be well, for after all we only want 'what is best for *you*.'

This last phrase is reiterated with great sincerity. It should not, however, be an excuse for that lack of sensitivity which forces a developing being into an incompatible mould. Humility and insight allow *and support* a freer choice.

These and similar influences lead us to acquire a conditioned well self. We sense that in some way we are gaining approval. We have chosen the right job, we have made a 'good' marriage, we have, or are working towards, a lovely home, lots of material possessions and the traditional 2.4 children. Conversely we may feel that we are approved only because we have rejected all these values and are suitably scruffy, ill-fed, rebellious and unemployed. Peer groups take over from parents as the approving authorities, and parents can project their own rebellions as well as their own conformities on to their children. In short, we only escape the conditioned well self when we take the courage to choose for ourselves.

The Sick Self

The conditioned well self easily becomes the sick self, leading us to pursue false values and false means of gaining self-respect. Too much conformity to the conditioned well self can lead us into mental, physical, emotional or spiritual illnesses and breakdowns. Often such breakdowns contain wisdom and force a reassessment of our lifestyle, life values and choices. Although such hiatuses are devastating to undergo, breakdown in the 'conditioned well self' can be a means of 'breaking through' to the true self.

Obviously it is altogether better if we can reassess the patterns when we are in a state of un-ease or dis-ease, rather than having to enter full sickness or breakdown to get insight. Helena (see page 49) found the right book at the right time, realised she needed to change, and set about doing so. Gaining insight is not always so straight-forward. Some of the ties which bind us to negative patterns, or the permissions we think we lack, are very powerful inhibitors indeed.

Dis-ease is an important early warning signal, which only too often is heeded insufficiently. At a physical level we get a headache and take an aspirin; we get a stronger headache and take two aspirins. We do not seek the reason behind the headache early enough. When we do investigate, the tendency is to concentrate too much on physical causes without looking to the mental, emotional or spiritual ones.

Too often when we are job-weary, bored, irritable, inexplicably over-tired or lose our sense of meaning, (other forms of dis-ease), we force ourselves on because we see no way of releasing conditioned values and expectations. At such times we are indeed vulnerable and 'dis-ease', if not noted or listened to, becomes either acute or chronic disease.

The True Well Self

We cannot overturn *all* the conditioned choices we have made, and will not always want to. But constant reassessment and attention to the things which really make our hearts sing are important to the well-being and nourishment of the true well self. The true well self blossoms and releases vitality, energy and positive all-round healthfulness into our lives when we are more conscious of the reasons which lie behind the compromises we have made and when we are open to modifying them progressively. When the true well self is honoured, then we follow the light and purpose of our higher selves as easily and naturally as a sunflower's face follows the sun.

The Inner Child

We may see, understand and accept all this at an intellectual level but, as we attempt to make modifications to our lives, all sorts of obstacles may unexpectedly appear. We try to alter the patterns, but they reassert themselves. The emotions are always more difficult to transform than the mind. Purely mental decisions or affirmations help to get the process in motion, but will not bring it to completion. Usually, at the basis of resistance to change lies the fear, neediness, uncertainty and suffering of the inner child.

Erudite works have been written on the psychological phenomenon of the inner child (see Bibliography). The following nutshell definition may be over-simplistic, but sets the scene sufficiently for the explorations which lie within the scope of this book.

During childhood it is almost inevitable that parents and teachers will misunderstand or misinterpret our behaviour and needs from time to time. If, for instance, a child is constantly deprived of the right kind of attention it may discover that being 'naughty' wins notice, and conclude that negative response and even punishment are better than no attention at all. In such a case the true needs of the child are not met. With growth into adulthood, an immature, unsatisfied inner part will live on as a needy and perhaps naughty, neglected and angry inner child. The adult's life and behaviour will be marked, at moments which may come as a surprise or embarrassment, by this autonomous aspect making itself known and felt.

A different response to lack of attention would be withdrawal and self-sufficiency, with resentment and deprivation lying beneath it. Then, in times of crisis, the inner child would cause the adult to 'split off', retreat into a world of his or her own and find it difficult to maintain an open emotional relationship.

Too many boundaries or punishments can lead to a cowed, fearful, over-conformist or imprisoned inner child – too few to one who is insecure or dangerously risk-taking. Too much richness in material things can lead to a 'spoiled' or insatiable inner child, – too little in the material sense can also produce an insatiable or hungry child. Too much emphasis on cleanliness can create an over-fastidious inner child or a dirty, messy one.

The needy aspects of the child within lead us to seek parenting and permission from others, often for much of our lives. We cannot truly empower ourselves to the making of free choices until we recognise the inner child's needs and take responsibility for healing these parts within ourselves. To make the process more complicated, until we gain fuller insights our own inner censor may reflect our parents' attitudes. Thus we may continue to punish and oppress the fearful, over-indulge the spoiled and undernourish the hungry children within. Such mechanisms are all part of the complexities of conditioning.

When we have children of our own, we may become replicas of our own parents or swing so thoroughly in the opposite direction as to create an undesirable polarisation. I was a child who had too many boundaries. As a parent I did not give my daughter enough – to the extent that she went through a period of feeling that I did not really care about her and her safety.

The work of cultivating the good inner parent and healing the hurts of our inner child is long-term but satisfying. It is a task which eventually leads to the clearest vision and release of the true self or seed. This is an area where self-help is very effective, but it should be noted that if the childhood difficulties were severe or overwhelming the help of a trained therapist could be needed.

Entelechy

So far the matter of the inner child has been mainly described as a psychological mechanism. The psychological and spiritual fields differ, but inter-relate: there is an important interface between them.

At that interface lies the concept of the true self. Psychologists study the uniqueness of each human individual, often without being able to arrive at any psychological definition. Hypotheses as to its nature inevitably lead us through the interface into metaphysical, spiritual or mystical realms where it is more natural to speak of a 'divine spark', or an 'inner blueprint'.

Plato spoke of a process which he called 'entelechy'. It is the power which directs an organism towards the fulfilment of its own intrinsic nature. Our difficulties, frustrations, fears, complexes and anxieties arise when there is conscious or unconscious denial of that intrinsic nature and when the process of entelechy is blocked or denied.

The Golden Child

Some Eastern systems of spiritual growth, including alchemy, make reference to the discovery or birth of a golden child or flower (see bibliography). When the obstacles along the path have been cleared, the tests passed and inner union with the divine accomplished, then this simple but wondrous essence presents itself. It is many things in one. It signifies inner creativity, linking with the higher self, a sense of communion with the divine, a firm inner knowing that there is a beneficent meaning and purpose to life, a renewed and renewable connection to the life-force and the joy of it.

Healing the inner child helps us to rediscover a sense of wonder. Without following a complex esoteric path we can meet an aspect of the inner child which is golden, alive – a harbinger of light, love and fun. Without being a Peter Pan, this child remains forever young and fresh. It is never downtrodden by life and embodies a wise innocence which can help us to achieve changes of perspective and find creative solutions to life's challenges.

Obedience

This word constantly recurs in spiritual and religious instruction and thought. For most of us it is also associated with being out of favour, with childhood and its rebellions, punishments and disciplines.

There is a tendency to see the higher self as demanding obedience and thus of being parental, judgemental or punishing. Rarely is the requirement of obedience aligned with the true self. When it is, it acquires grace and beauty. Subjection of will or subservience play no part in finding the freedom to be fully obedient to who or what we truly are.

Forgiveness

This too is a spiritually connected concept. Although a familiar word, it is still difficult to define. It is a process which goes beyond pardoning, excusing or compassion. When it is achieved, the one who forgives and the one who is forgiven enter into a dual 'state of grace'. A deep mutual understanding occurs. Hurts which have been received and grudges borne are completely released.

Matters requiring forgiveness usually centre on betrayal of trust. Yet trust is an expectation, and sometimes we impose its burden on those who have neither asked us to do so nor are ready and able to carry it. Of course we need to nurture and nourish relationships which have trust at their core, but we can only trust each other when we have found how to trust ourselves.

Acceptance has to be reached before forgiveness is achieved. This involves recognising that somewhere in the scheme of things we are each other's teachers. Even betraying and being betrayed are lessons. When this insight is fully embraced, forgiveness is no longer a problem. If the lesson had to be learned, then there is nothing to forgive in its teacher.

Self-forgiveness is often the heaviest task of all. It is difficult to be the instrument which inflicts hurt on others and difficult to accept that we sometimes step so unwarily into life's tangles and traps.

Karma and Forgiveness

An understanding of karma can help in enabling forgiveness. Beyond the theory that karma is over-simplistic – like the Judaic law, 'an eye for an eye and a tooth for a tooth' – lies the belief that, as we recognise the effects of the actions we make, so we choose ways in which to redeem our mistakes or make retribution for them.

These choices are made by our higher selves. As an incarnation takes place, the factors which the incoming being will meet have already been overseen. These include the psychological environment and therefore most of the obstacles of conditioning which will be experienced. In life, a frequent mistake is to assume that, because we have been conditioned, no matter how unhappy that conditioning makes us it must be 'meant' or fated and we should therefore bow before it. This is one of the factors which leads us into conflicts with obedience and can make us feel compelled to honour false gods.

Instead, the choice of our psychological environment is mostly about making our life lessons more conscious. As explained on page 43, some of the limitations chosen give us boundaries. Others are selected because we want to make amends or retribution for past mistakes. Yet others are there to make us more aware of our strengths.

When an obstacle offers us a constructive challenge we come out on the other side of it with more self-knowledge, more strength, more creativity and more courage than if the obstacle had not been encountered. We tend to get stuck in the area of 'retribution' and all too readily see obstacles as confinements and restrictions. The consciousness of the retributive balances we need to make comes from natural reactions to the given environment.

Brought up by ascetic parents, we may wholeheartedly

and with conscious devotion take their principles on board. Alternatively we may take them on board but be uncomfortable or inconsistent with them; throw them aside, but feel guilt with every act of seeming self-indulgence; or be moved to find a truly middle way. Whichever reaction, the underlying message for the present lifetime is most likely to be about redeeming an incarnation governed by excess. The first and last reactions listed here are probably the most healthy. The others show within them the struggle to come to terms with choice and self-responsibility, the pains of overcoming conditioning or the need for 'permission' in order to be free to move forward.

In the context of forgiveness, this limited example can show that there is no question of being trapped into a response such as 'I find it difficult to forgive my parents for having deprived me of material comforts' once the parental environment is recognised as having been chosen for the evolutionary teaching it can give. The inner child may feel deprived, but recognition that there is an alternative angle of perception makes it easier to rally the forces which will heal the child.

Spiritually speaking, the things which oppose us help us to ask the right questions about our lives and thence to make decisions based on those questions. The fatalistic response of '*Che sarà, sarà,* whatever, will be, will be' leaves out the important factors of love, joy, choice, hope and creativity. It assumes that the whole of life on earth has the characteristics of a 'life sentence', rather than being a gift of embodied life-force full of positive opportunity.

Cutting the Ties that Bind

As human beings, we seek close relationships and long to find positive ties of love and commitment. Yet, if commitment becomes negative or love possessive, the ties that bind (see Bibliography) begin to feel like chains of bondage.

There are ties created by conditioning, emotional blackmail, false or divided loyalties, and unreasonable expectations of, or from, ourselves and others. These affect every aspect of interpersonal and intrapersonal relationships. Once their existence is recognised, effective cutting or dissolving of them is aided by visualisation and prayer.

Because of the value we put on ties, the prospect of cutting even those which are subtly destructive is daunting. We collude with, and feed from, many negative patterns. Though we crave freedom, we often fear it. Though we picture ourselves as achievers, we may realise at the same time that success is hard for us to handle. We have secret investments in the things which prevent or hold back our forward progress. Negative patterns have 'benefits', and before we dissolve them we need insights into exactly what nourishment we are gaining from them.

Once we realise that we can make free and responsible choices, we do not need to hide behind 'excuses' to explain why we didn't pursue a particular pathway, opportunity or goal: 'Having Mother to look after meant I could never travel'; 'I didn't move to that better job in the North of England because of disrupting the children's schooling'; 'I didn't want to "upset the applecart"'; 'My wife couldn't have coped with the pressures'; 'Life has asked a lot of sacrifices of me on my road to the top, but I *had* to do it – I *had* to prove myself.'

These comments are intrinsically sad because they imply frustration by, or bondage to, others. They do not express responsible choice. Rephrased, they give a completely different impression:

'I've found it such a privilege to look after Mother that I decided to do it wholeheartedly. Giving up travel was a small price to pay'; 'If I'd moved to that job in the North of England everything might have changed – I was happy with a less glamourous post, focusing my attention on the family and the children's schooling'; 'Everyone, including myself, was happy with life – I wouldn't have exchanged what I had for anything'; 'I couldn't have coped with the pressures and would have been afraid of the changes it might bring to our relationship'; 'I really wanted to get to the top. I paid a price but I've got what I wanted.'

The second group of statements is open and honest. They contain much less evidence of subtle, collusive, emotional bondage. The people making them would be in positive, non-apologetic charge of their lives.

Positive cutting of the ties that bind means that we release more energy into our lives, cut out negative collusions, provide opportunity for emotional climates to change and leave space for the true, higher nature of our relationships to become clear. The exercises starting on page 68 include suggestions for cutting the ties that bind. But before moving on to these I hand over to Gildas to speak on issues related to this chapter and particularly about the remedial zone of the astral plane.

GILDAS

The largest and most varied of the subtle planes which exist beyond the physical or material plane on which you dwell is the astral.

It ranges from its lower regions, peopled with thought forms, through beautiful colour landscapes to temples of light and healing. It is the plane which you most often visit in your dreams. It contains that area of light so often remembered by those who have had a near death experience. Here, in dreams or through mediumship, you meet with loved ones who have died to the physical world. In its upper reaches, where it blends with the feeling and mental planes, you meet with your true guides, helpers and beings of light from the angelic realms.

In the 'between life' state many choose to 'work' in some area of the astral plane.

The healing and light temples are formed of light and colour and geometric pattern. You visit them in a similar way to that in which you would visit an earth temple or beautiful building.

There is also a whole area of the astral plane given over to healing and remedial activity. I refer to this, perhaps somewhat unromantically, as 'the remedial zone'.

You do not have to die to visit the remedial zone. You can do so in dreams or, more consciously, with the aid of visualisation or guided journeys. Many things happen here. Healing energies abound. Many healers, helpers and workers are busy here. In your sleep time you may come to this zone for help or healing or in order to help others. Many of you do spiritual 'work' in your sleep.

Much of the work of the remedial zone is concerned with the healing of children and relationships. This includes healing the inner child. These vulnerable parts of yourselves are like separate universes, and they are able to come to the remedial zone for care and healing even before you begin to work consciously with them yourselves. This happens mostly during sleep. But if the inner child is very needy or split off from the person to whom it belongs, then it may come to reside in this remedial zone. Although it will be looked after and given healing, it still needs to grow and be integrated into the person to whom it rightly belongs. The split off inner child cannot be fully healed until it has been recognised and claimed. Thus, when you work with your inner child you also work on the remedial zone.

Other children here are young souls, unable as yet to take on full incarnation, or perhaps traumatised by a difficult experience during a primary incarnation. Children who die young also come to this place for a period of adjustment. Abortion or death during the gestation period usually leave a slightly disorientated personality spark, which is brought to the remedial zone for healing and reorientation.

The healing sanctuaries here are peopled by many kinds of worker, including angels, guides and discarnate healers. Some of these sanctuaries are dedicated to particularly helpful archetypes. For instance, there are the sanctuaries of the divine mother and divine father. When you find it difficult to be a good parent to yourself and your inner child, you may bring the inner child to these temples and together learn what is required to help your growth and healing so that the golden child can be more easily released or accessible.

All these activities have connections with karma, which is synonymous with growth and evolution. Every plane of consciousness helps the learning process. The more you learn to be aware of at least the existence of the subtle planes, the more you can be active and aware in your own evolution, not only for the present incarnate personality, but for the totality of your soul.

A time is coming when the experience of earth will no longer be an experience as difficult or seemingly split off from the other dimensions as it is for you now. The nature of karma will change, so that its emphasis is more fully on redemption and transcendence and less on repayment and the making of direct and harsh retribution.

When you work on forgiveness, particularly of self, you help to hasten this happier phase of human incarnation. One of the problems with forgiveness is that you so often feel guilty when you are unable to forgive. You also seem to find it difficult to accept being forgiven. When you are conscious of a wrong you have done to another, and that wrong is freely forgiven or understood, then you tend to hold on to guilt.

Try to reflect that in the great scheme of things everything has its place. When you speak of forgiveness try dividing the word, thus: forgiven-ness. Then, perhaps, you will have less difficulty in transposing the immediately personal into context with the wider. In the final analysis all is already forgiven.

Exercises Relating to this Chapter

Guided Journey to the River of Childhood

Sit or lie in a comfortable but symmetrically balanced position. Make sure that you will be undisturbed, that

you have a blanket for warmth and crayons and paper
on hand for any recording you wish to do.

Be aware of the rhythm of your breathing . . .
gradually bring that rhythm into your heart centre or
chakra. Travel on the heart energy into your inner
landscape . . . Find yourself in the meadow . . . Awaken
your inner senses, so that you can see the objects and
colours around you . . . hear the sounds . . . smell the
fragrances . . . touch the textures . . . and taste the tastes
. . . Ask for your inner wise presence to accompany you
or to bless this journey, and make sure that you have
with you any talisman or amulet you wish to take . . .

From the meadow take the path which leads to the
landing-stage from which you departed on your journey
to the source of the river . . .

Sit for a while on the bank, near the landing-stage
and your river boat, in order to reflect . . .

The river of childhood is upstream from where you
are now (how far upstream will depend somewhat on
your present chronological age) . . . When you took
your journey to the source, you were asked to note
areas of the river which you would like to revisit . . .
Review the possible choices now . . . You might want to
explore a backwater, a whirlpool or turgid area of your
river in order to understand more about your life's
obstacles . . . Remember that you can repeat this
journey as often as you wish, each time making different
choices . . . Therefore, on this occasion, choose one more
difficult or mysterious area and also one area of beauty,
sunshine and lightheartedness where there might be the
possibility of capturing the essence of the 'golden
child' . . .

When you know where you want to go, you may
travel in the same river vessel which took you to the
source . . . You may decide to walk along the river

banks . . . You may 'will' yourself to be immediately
there . . . You may choose a different river vessel . . .

Travel first to the more difficult area of your choice
. . . When you arrive, explore it as fully as you wish . . . As
you do so, note whether you are the adult observing,
perhaps watching scenes from childhood as though on a
film . . . or whether you *become* the child you once were,
reliving a part of your childhood's journey . . . As you
explore, what memories reawaken for you? . . . What seem
to be the most important factors in these memories? . . . Do
not push yourself to remember trauma . . . Ask your psyche
to be gentle in its revelations . . . accept whatever surfaces,
even though it may not seem to be fresh material . . . even
though there may be no new perspective or disclosure . . .
Your talisman is with you, and your guardian angel and
inner wise presence will answer your call . . . (Take ten to
fifteen minutes for this exploration, feeling free to return to
the meadow and thence to your normal everyday world, if
you should wish . . .)

When you are ready to move on, remember your
mode of travel . . . You are now going to visit a beautiful
part of the river . . . some place associated with positive
childhood experience . . . A place where the sun always
shines . . . where harmony abounds . . . When you arrive,
enter into the spirit of play . . . Explore this part of the
river with a sense of wonder . . . Are you led to some
specific memory or memories? . . . Perhaps a golden
child will appear to accompany you and lead you . . .
Perhaps you will become aware of nature spirits or
fairies around you . . . Perhaps the essence of your
guardian angel or a guide will dance in and out of these
sunlit memories with you . . . (Again take ten to fifteen
minutes for this exploration . . .)

Finally return to the landing-stage . . . from there to
your meadow . . . to the rhythm of your breathing in

your heart centre . . . to awareness of your physical body in
your own everyday physical surroundings . . . Imagine a
cloak of white light with a hood surrounding you . . . Take
crayons, pens and paper and record your journey . . .

Reflection on Your Journey

THE DIFFICULT AREA OF YOUR CHOICE
Which difficult area did you choose?
How do you see the symbolism of your choice? Was it a
backwater? Weedy patch? Muddy pool? Whirlpool?
Rapid? Patch of turgid water? Dangerous current?
Something else? Which part of yourself did you meet here?
How were you dressed? (Even if you chose to observe from
a distance, how were you dressed?) What was your feeling,
and the feeling quality of the whole scene?

What sort of memory did the area of your choice trigger?
As you visited this place on your inner river, did you
have any definite memories of periods or incidents in
your young life? Were there specific causes of your
unhappinesses, or were you subject to overall
misunderstanding? Were you unseen? Unheard?
Unnoticed?

Were you alone or were others with you?
Did you experience the presence of childhood friends?
Parents? Extended family? Adult family friends? What
was their role? Were they supportive during a time of
crisis, or was the crisis, trauma or unhappiness mostly
activated by others?

What age were you?
If you can pinpoint your age during whatever you
experienced in this memory, maybe you can decide what

outer factor it was that changed things. Did the influence of that outer factor continue, lessen or intensify?

THE AREA OF SUNSHINE, BEAUTY AND LIGHTHEARTEDNESS
What sort of area was this?
What quality did you experience here? Was it that quality or features of the landscape itself which made it so captivating?

Did you have memories of specific incidents or periods during your childhood?
If so, what was it that made them special? The presence of some specific factor? The presence of a particular person or persons? Had you been given something special? Had you been noticed, included or rewarded in an especially sensitive or significant way?

Did you experience closeness to nature, nature spirits, animals or the natural kingdom?
Were you encouraged to appreciate natural beauty when you were a child? From what age were you aware that your 'heart could sing'?

Was there a golden child in your visualisation or experience?
If so, try to keep this image vivid, vibrant and alive. In meditation or reverie, revisit this place and try to make a stronger relationship with the inner, golden child. What do you feel the golden child has to teach you or could help you with at this point in your outer, adult life?

Cutting the Ties that Bind

Reflect on the quality of your relationship with parents and others (Even if your parents are now dead). Reread the section on cutting the ties on page 64.

If there are ties to be cut, select one of the following methods, or use each of them alternately. To be effective, tie-cutting visualisations usually have to be repeated frequently (daily or every other day) for about a month. They should then be repeated about once a week until a difference is noticed, and thereafter used from time to time as reinforcement or if similar situations or old-style reactions recur. Getting a friend, partner or counsellor to 'witness' your intention in cutting the ties can be a great help. If you want to cut ties with more than one person, make a separate visualisation for each. If there are more than two people or situations to deal with, first select the two most vital ones to work on. Start new visualisations only after you have worked for approximately two months with the original ones.

METHOD 1

Visualise yourself standing in a circle of light. The person with whom you wish to cut the ties is also standing in a circle of light, facing you. Your circles of light are touching each other or even slightly overlapping. There are greyish pulsating cords running from some of your vital centres or chakras to the corresponding centres in the other person. (These most commonly run from root chakra to root chakra, sacral to sacral, solar plexus to solar plexus.) Move back so that your circles no longer overlap; now put an extra circle of violet light around your existing circle and then a fine circle of silver light around that. Do the same for the person with whom you are intending to cut the ties. Emphasise the space between your circles.

Now, visualise the grey cords withering and dropping away into the space between you. Let the space between you become a river of light. The river of light takes the cords into its flow, filling them with light and washing them away to the sea.

Ask your guardian angel for a blessing, and ask the guardian angel of the other person to do the same for them. As you bask in the light of blessing, try to become aware of the lessons that you and the other person have taught or mirrored to each other and to be thankful for those lessons.

Feel your own space firmly around you as you let the visualisation fade.

METHOD 2

Visualise yourself standing opposite the person with whom you wish to cut the ties. Visualise a symbol of peace which you would wish to offer this person, and see them holding it. See yourself holding a replica of this symbol. As you hold the symbols, be aware of the lessons you have reflected for each other.

As in method 1, see the grey and pulsating cords which bind running between your vital areas or chakras. Visualise a shaft of silver light, which flashes three times between you, melting away the cords and leaving you free.

See a pathway of light behind you and behind the person with whom you are cutting the ties. See each of you turn, with your symbol of peace, to follow your own distinctive path. As you walk away, the shaft of light appears to define a boundary. In future neither of you can cross that boundary except at the other's invitation. (This method is particularly good where there has been a sense of 'invasion' from another person.)

The Inner Child and the Remedial Zone

1. Collect some photographs from your childhood. As you study them, try to connect with your inner child and its behaviours, fears, resentments and needs.

2. Before you sleep, ask to be able to take your inner child to the remedial zone of the astral plane for healing.

3. Visualise a temple of rose-coloured light – the sanctuary of the divine mother. Imagine taking to this sanctuary any aspect of your inner child which needs healing. Imagine the divine mother giving your inner parent a blessing, so that you can work more effectively and patiently with your inner child.

4. Visualise a temple of soft green light – the sanctuary of the divine father. (Repeat instructions as for 3, above.)

Your Karmic Tasks

Reflect on the obstacles you have met in your life. Viewing them symbolically, try to get a sense of the direction they have caused you to take and the lessons they have taught you. (Persistence? Surrender? Acceptance? Moderation?) Use your imagination to sense how this life may be a foil, balance or polarity to imbalances or excesses in a previous lifetime.

Entelechy

Breathing the heart breath, as at the beginning of a guided journey (see page 16), meditatively seek an image or symbol for your seed or potential. Keeping the meditative space around you, draw or paint this image.

Now, seek a second image or symbol which represents the 'becoming' of the seed. When it has grown to perfect fruition what will it be? Meditatively draw or paint this image also. Use your images for reflection and inspiration. Do not strive to understand them mentally.

Case History: The River of Childhood

Vincent was worried about the extent of his smoking and drinking and the effects they were beginning to have on his health, vitality, efficiency and ability to make relationships. A trained teacher, he had been working successfully in a tough London junior school for three years. But now he felt himself to be on the edge of a breakdown. He was depressed, and had started waking late and letting down his colleagues and class of children by not appearing on time.

He had had several relationships, none of which had been long-term. This worried him, as marriage and children were high in his priorities. Each of his girlfriends had accused him of failing to see them as people in their own right. At the same time they saw him as intense and over-possessive. Despairing of 'getting it right', he had begun to spend a lot of his free time in pubs or wine bars and now felt he was in danger of serious addiction.

When Vincent visited the river of childhood, he went first to a place where his river was muddy, murky and had dangerous eddies and currents. As he contemplated this part of the river, he attained a new insight into some aspects of his childhood. He was one of four children, with one brother and two sisters. He was an unplanned, 'late' child. When he was born, the sister next in age to himself was sixteen. He had not really been welcomed and so had grown up with a sense of being superfluous.

One of the memories which came as he contemplated the muddy part of his river was from the period between being two years old to starting school at the age of five. The rest of his family were adults, with their own lives to lead and busy morning routines. His mother had gone back to her teaching career and there was a daily house-keeper. Vincent would stay in bed, out of the way, whilst everyone went off to work. He would get a quick kiss from his mother as she left, and then wait until it was 'convenient' for the housekeeper to get him up and give him his breakfast. This was often quite late. He did not rebel as some children might, but became passive and sleepy.

At weekends and holidays there was a contrast. Vincent became the centre of attention and responded by becoming very clinging and demanding. Perhaps a sense of guilt about the weekday neglect caused the adults to indulge his every whim.

No wonder women found Vincent difficult! With them he was demanding and intense. Away from them he would cut off and leave them to make all the contacts and connections.

Vincent had a very sad inner child who had never learned to play. During our work together he also found the angry child and the angry adult. These became positive aspects, because they were fighting for Vincent's self-respect. Gradually he realised that he had become a teacher only because he came from a family of teachers. Initially, something had spurred him to 'sail a good ship' as far as his career was concerned, but the hidden currents had eventually dragged him into a pattern of confusion.

The happy place on Vincent's river was a grove of

trees at the waterside. He revealed that he loved wood as a substance and had a collection of different polished woods. He loved to handle the varied textures and examine the colours and grains brought out by turning and polishing. He decided to learn the art of wood turning, and eventually changed his career to take this up professionally.

Wood turning made him feel that he was in contact with his true essence – an experience so healing that he was able to give up his smoking and excessive drinking quite easily. Working with his anger and his inner children enabled Vincent to achieve more balance in his expectations of others. He felt that one of his karmic tasks related to achieving a balanced self-sufficiency.

At about the time that he really began to feel more relaxed about his expectations of life and relationships, Vincent met the woman to whom he is now happily married. She is a successful book illustrator. They have two children and live in wooded countryside. Vincent's workshop is in a converted barn nearby. The lovely bowls and decorative pieces which he makes have become well known and are in great demand.

5

The River of Light

The knowledge of man is as the waters, some
descending from above and some springing from
beneath; the one informed by the light of nature,
the other inspired by divine revelation.

FRANCIS BACON

*Angels, archangels and guides in daily life . . . The art of
obtaining and following effective spiritual help and guidance
. . . Prayer . . Invocation . . . Meditation . . .*

Angels

Belief in, and teaching about, angels and archangels is
common to the major religions. Even in the Christian
religion a study of angels brings a welcome burst of light,
since the presence of these wondrous beings modifies the
effect of a heavily patriarchal and anthropomorphic god
and his moral and judgemental 'hang-ups'. Considering
angels takes us from divine principles to light and laugh-
ter, from the miracle of infinity to the precision with
which each one of us is seen and cared for in the scheme
of the universe.

Ancient esoteric teachings from Zoroastrian and He-
braic roots yield traditional, comprehensive and fascinating information about the angelic hierarchies. The discarnate teaching guides of our time indicate that the angelic

forces are seeking a more personal and direct relationship with us. Angels can teach us about the nature of
light and help us to 'lighten' ourselves, our lives and
the earth.

The word 'angel' means 'messenger'. Each angel is a
message or mirror of one of the infinite facets of the
divine. Their stream of consciousness is at one with the
divine. They will never incarnate, and we shall never be
angels. Human and angelic evolution are different
streams of consciousness.

Fairies, elementals, nature spirits and devas are part of
the same energy stream as angels. There is a hierarchical
progression, from the life-force which helps plants and
minerals to grow, to angels, archangels and members of
the highest ranks of the heavenly hosts.

Guardian angels

Guardian angels have already been mentioned (see
page 45). They are the first rank of angels, and evolve
from the devic life streams. When our higher selves
make the decision to set an incarnation in motion, then
a guardian angel is born. Thus from the moment that
each of our incarnations is planned we are accompanied by a guardian angel. This being will preside at
our physical birth and accompany us, eventually,
through the journey of death. It will not interfere with
our free will, but will travel beside us, protect us
when we are in danger, hold us when we go too near
the edge of the precipice, witness our joy and comfort
our tears.

Many children are aware of their guardian angels,
but this is one of the sensitivities of consciousness
which we easily lose in our preoccupations with
the mundane.

Guides

A guardian angel is not the same as a discarnate guide. Guides are on the human stream of consciousness, have been incarnate and may incarnate again. There is more reference to them on pages 84–6.

The Angelic Hierarchy

There is only space here for a précis of the different levels of angelic beings. There are three realms of angels, each divided into three degrees. The first realm, closest to the divine, are heavenly counsellors, followed by heavenly governors and then messengers.

Heavenly counsellors

Seraphim hold the highest rank in the angelic army. They conduct the music of the spheres. They keep the right balance of sound and alignment of movement between the planets and other heavenly bodies.

Cherubim are guardians of light, particularly that which comes from the stars. They enable mystical experience by making a bridge or transforming the intensity of direct divine light so that we can safely experience it in our incarnate, embodied state.

Thrones oversee the life of each of the planets. The major angel of the earth is a throne, but the moon also has its throne, as do Jupiter, Venus and so on.

Heavenly governors

Dominions give advice, support and counsel to the lower groups in the angelic hierarchy.

Virtues help response to prayer and requests for healing by focusing suitable concentrations of divine energy into specific areas or for specific individuals.

Powers look after the keeping of the akashic records. They inspire human conscience and oversee the rhythms of birth and death.

Messengers

Principalities give guardianship to nations, large groups and cities.

Archangels help us to interpret divine principles. They overlight all aspects of human endeavour. The ones most commonly named are Michael, Gabriel, Uriel and Raphael. When we understand more about their areas of expertise we can invoke them to bring blessing, safety and protection to our daily lives.

It is usual to speak of angels as 'he', and many of them have names traditionally given to men and boys. Women often find this masculine orientation difficult to accept. When necessary, I use the traditional 'he', to avoid clumsiness of style and because our only other neuter in English is 'it' which, again used constantly, becomes awkward. Angels are beyond gender and fully balanced in masculine and feminine principle. Like humans, some use more of the masculine principle for their work and some more of the feminine.

Michael's name means: 'Who is like the divine?' He is guardian of the direction of the north, of night-time, of the season of winter, of the element of air, our spirits and our dreams. The colour which helps us to link with, or invoke, him is blue. He is often portrayed as the one who wields the sword in order to slaughter the dragons of evil – but even angels and their purposes evolve. In 1950 the Pope declared Michael to be the patron of policemen. If policemen are seen as keepers of the peace, then this is in line with seeing Michael as a guardian rather than a warrior. He has the power to transform dragons and enable them to breathe the fire of life into the feminine principle. He blesses cooperation and reconciliation, and helps us to learn to live in peace with others. He teaches us to ask the right question at the right time.

Gabriel's name means: 'The divine is my strength.' He is the guardian of the south, noon, summer, water and our emotions. His 'link' colour is green. Gabriel is the angel of revelation and hope (he was the angel who told Mary she was pregnant with Jesus). He gives especial blessing and protection to women and children, and helps to bring healing to dysfunctional families.

Uriel's name means: 'The light and fire of the divine.' He is the guardian of the east, the rising sun, morning, spring, alchemy, the mind and the element of fire. His link colour is yellow. Uriel overlights the worlds of science, economics, politics, political reform and medical research. He blesses social equality and helps us to find our direction in life.

Raphael's name means: 'The divine has healed.' He is the guardian of the west, twilight, evening, autumn, healing and the element of earth. His link colour is red. He blesses growth, transformation and all forms of healing, from surgery to herbalism and the 'laying on of hands'. He brings comfort and protection to all who are physically, spiritually, emotionally or mentally ill.

Angels, including guardian angels, protect and inspire us at very direct and personal levels. They are those members without rank in the angelic army who adapt to being more playfully named. Many readers will know the delightful packs of 'angel cards' which originated at the Findhorn Foundation. They carry such names as 'Delight', 'Trust', 'Play' and 'Humour', and help us to see how we can invoke angelic qualities and protection into daily life.

Some of my favourite angels are the 'car parking angels' who, invoked and given fair warning, always manage to find me a parking space or meter. Gildas insists that angels want to help us in daily life and that it is not irreverent or nonsensical to involve them in such mundane activities as car parking.

Lucifer is a part of any chronicle of angels. He is the traditional 'fallen' angel, often thought of as seductive and evil. Another way to look at Lucifer is to see him as the one who follows the human journey most closely. His name means 'light', and with this light he shows us the darker side of things, the shadow, from which we learn the lessons of knowledge and experience. If the choice of human beings to separate from the divine and take the journey of knowledge can be seen as a 'fall', then Lucifer made the sacrifice of 'falling' with us. He communicates the conditions of earth to the other angels and helps to show where modification is needed.

Guides

As previously stated, guides are on the human stream of evolution. Our 'true' or higher guides have usually reached a point in that evolution where they do not need to reincarnate. They may choose to do so for reasons of service to humanity, but it is unneccessary for their own evolutionary experience.

Each of us has a personal guide, just as we have a guardian angel. Guides watch over, advise and help us. They build a bridge for us between the different planes of reality, enabling us to acquire a greater consciousness of all the more subtle layers, aspects and forms of life.

They may be there mainly as personal companions, or they may require our help in fulfilling a broader mission to collective humanity. (Gildas says that his task is to reach a wide audience. Part of the commitment of my higher self for this lifetime was to be his 'channel', 'link', amanuensis or cooperating partner.)

Guides have different main areas of interest or expertise. If their mission to humanity is wide, they will focus on teaching, healing, inspiration, aiding research, helping interplanetary communication or any combination of these.

At the soul level, we belong to families and groups. Our guides are usually from within our soul group, and we will have met them in previous incarnations. (For more information about soul groups and guides see *A Message of Love*. For fuller instruction on guidance see *A Question of Guidance*. Details of both these titles can be found in the Bibliography.)

Guides do not see each other as Red Indians, Tibetan priests, French monks, priestesses, sisters of mercy or temple dancers. Such guises, in which we usually perceive them, are really 'trappings' which they assume to help us in recognising and relating to them. The choice of 'costume' will usually be related to a meeting we have had with them in another lifetime. We have to be careful not to 'limit' them by our historical curiosity about the personalities in which they appear. (See also page 4.)

In the state where incarnation is no longer necessary, beings have a less defined form than that which we have on earth. Personality and distinct individuality are no longer either necessary or important. They are diffuse essences. Their communication with each other is mainly through thought waves or vibrations.

Many well known guides choose a masculine form in which to appear, but there are many female guides.

Again, in essence, guides are beyond gender. If they have a masculine principle task like teaching to accomplish, they tend to appear as males. If their task is more from the feminine principle, as with certain areas of healing, then they come through in female form.

How to Obtain and Follow Spiritual Guidance

Accepting that there are hosts of angelic and discarnate beings ready to help us is one thing. Learning to recognise and use that help as a normal, natural part of our daily lives is another.

Imagining direct contact with angels or guides may cause us to feel fear, awe, embarrassment, unworthiness or a sense of the ridiculous. There is a doctor in Holland who always asks his patients, 'Have you ever seen an angel?' The number of people who answer in the affirmative is overwhelming. It is a compliment to the doctor that his patients feel relaxed enough with him to describe their experiences. I suspect that if I were asked such a question by a doctor I might assume he was doubting my sanity!

Extra-sensory perceptions shake, fascinate and confuse us. Did it really happen or not? One moment it is there, the next gone. There is nothing tangible, no proof we can show to others, only a feeling quality which may be overlaid with a sense of eeriness. Yet, like the Dutch doctor, I am convinced that most people have more extra-sensory perception than they may care to own to or speak about.

We must endeavour to forget the eerie and the ghostly. Angels are beneficent presences. Guides are not ghosts, but beings inhabiting another plane, who are as connected with the human experience as we are. None of these presences, angels or guides, will impose themselves in a way which we find disconcerting. If you are afraid of *seeing* them, yet want to be reassured that they are there, eventually they will give a sense of their comforting presence, without imposition or invasion.

If you long to see and feel other presences but have no success, it is probably because your expectations are not 'loose' enough. Perception of other planes is not the same as seeing concrete reality. The subtle is real and vivid, but by its very nature it is not concrete. It moves and vibrates – it does not stay constant in the same way that the chair by the window stays there unless it is moved.

There are many ways of perceiving the subtle, and we have to get to know and accept 'our' way. The manner in which I perceive and communicate with Gildas is not a 'model'. This is a world in which there are examples but no models. It is a world where the subjective experience is of foremost importance. If you are too set on the way you want it to be, then you can block the way it is for you. Every 'sensitive' whom I have met has a different way of 'seeing' and 'hearing'. There are similarities, but each relationship with angels or guides is unique.

Acting 'as if'

The simplest way to become more aware of angels and guides is to 'act as if'. Begin to speak to your guardian angel or your guide. Tell them of your needs, your thoughts, your fears, your joys. Do not expect them to know everything without being told, to be able to fulfil your every need without its being expressed. Particularly do not project on to them the idea that they know everything that is 'good for you'.

Write them letters, speak to them mentally or aloud (the

latter preferably when you are alone!). Articulating your needs and hopes enables guides and angels to do their part to cause positive synchronicity to occur in your life. You may not immediately be able to have a two-way dialogue with your 'other-level' friends and guardians, but you will be surprised to find how often articulating what you want increases the number of times you meet the right person at the right time, pick up the right book and turn it to the right page, or get your needs met in an unexpected way.

Take the simple example of the car parking angels. All you are asking for is synchronicity. When you ask, it happens. When you forget or are negative about it, difficulties arise.

If you persevere with seeking guidance or angelic contact, eventually you will receive direct messages. These may come in precise words, even if only key-words, in symbols, in pictures or through an inner know-ing. Guides will tend to speak or commune at greater length and in greater detail. Angels will let you feel the caress of their wings, remove the fear from your heart or mind, make you aware of a colour or cause a gift to come to you. Their spoken messages are usually very brief.

There are many ways to make contact with the helpers from other worlds. Some step-by-step suggestions are given on pages 89–98.

Prayer, invocation, ritual and meditation are all impor-tant factors in helping the connections that are made to be as clear as possible.

Prayer

In defining prayer, I cannot do better than quote from Chambers English Dictionary:

pray – to ask earnestly (for); to entreat; to express

one's desires to, or commune with, a god or some spiritual power – to ask earnestly and reverently, as in worship, to supplicate; to present as a prayer; to render, get, put or cause to be, by praying.

prayer – one who prays; the act of praying; entreaty; a petition to, or communing with, a god or spiritual power; the wish put forward or the words used; a form used or intended for use in praying; public worship; a time set aside for worship in a family, school etc.

Many of us have reservations about prayer, perhaps because of family worship, school assemblies and having to learn long passages from the prayer books of a particular religion. Some people see prayer as reserved for direct access to God, and may still be uncertain about the relationship, particularly of guides, to God or the divine (Gildas speaks about this on page 94).

The attitude of prayer is ideally one of reverence for, trust in, and involvement with, the laws of the universe. It is the dialogue through which we make known our needs, our appreciation of natural laws and and that which we also have to offer. It is not the fawning abasement of the humble penitent sinner, whining self-condemnation and deprecation in return for whatever crumbs of favour or restraint in punishment the Almighty deigns to hand out.

It would be a mistake to pray, in the strictly religious sense, directly to a guide or angel, but it is perfectly congruent to involve their help in making our lives reverent and prayerful.

Invocation

Again the Chambers Dictionary's definition of invocation is comprehensive:

The act or the form of invoking or addressing in prayer or supplication; an appellation under which one is invoked; any formal invoking of the blessing or help of a god or saint, etc.; an opening prayer in a public religious service or in the Litany; a call for inspiration from a Muse or other deity as at the beginning of a poem; an incantation or calling up of a spirit; a call or summons.

Ideally an invocation should be a voicing aloud, naming the being or the forces which we call upon for help. To make proper invocation we must not be too meek. We must believe in our right to make that invocation and in the willingness of that which we invoke to come to our aid, inspiration or service.

When healing, I always make a simple and usually silent invocation: 'I invoke the aid and presence of the angels of light and love and healing.' This focuses my mind and intent and affirms my identity as a healer. I am immediately aware, also, of a sense of these presences giving their blessing. I am sure that they are present at any channelling of healing, whether named and called or not, but the act of invocation makes a bridge of awareness. It increases the ability of subtle presences to make their energy available to us in a form which is more directly interactive with the physical plane.

It is important, therefore, to name our angels and guides, even if the names we give them are sometimes mundane or humorous. The names of the most widely known archangels have been given. The angels, or angelic energies without rank or title in the hosts, respond to almost any name we wish to give them and will come to our aid for very specific purposes. The angel of punctuality or wakefulness will help us when we have difficulty in being on time or alert. The angel of tidiness will help us to maintain a balance of order. The angel of work will help us to carry out our daily tasks with a positive attitude. The angel of companionship will help when we are lonely. The angel of hope will come to our aid when we are depressed or without hope.

Our guardian angels are always with us, but even with them the connection is strengthened when we remember to make invocation to them. It is up to us to name our needs, and thus to name and invoke our angels. Studying the areas of expertise of the archangels and invoking them, according to our need or sphere of interest, will empower us, aid our sense of purpose and help us to play our role in the cast of the great, unfolding human drama.

It is not so easy to know the names of our guides. Usually we have to wait until they tell, or cause us to be told, how they wish to be known. When seeking a better guidance connection or asking for help before their names are known we can still specify: 'I invoke my personal guide', 'I invoke my true guide', 'I invoke my higher guide', 'I invoke my teaching guide', 'I invoke my healing guide.'

Ritual

Here the dictionary definition is less comprehensive, but these extracts are worth quoting: 'the manner of performing divine service, or a book containing it; a body or code of ceremonies; an often repeated series of actions; the performance of rites; ceremonial.'

I have used the word 'bridge' several times in describing the presence and purpose of angels and guides. It is important to recognise that we do need a bridge between the different worlds. Just as electricity needs a transformer before it is suitable for domestic use, so naked spiritual energy needs to assume a form which is more in tune with our earthliness. Properly trained priests and priestesses perfected and strengthened their own psychic sensitivities or 'energy bodies' and led dedicated lives so that they could stand 'nearer to the flame' than those who were ungifted, unstrengthened or untrained. Through careful use of ritual they would enable the masses to attain mystical insights when required for special ceremonies or rites of celebration or passage.

Today, even within the Church, most of our rituals are dead or dying. We have handed many of them over to the state. The words are said, but the spirit is lacking. There are no protected environments in which we can train and strengthen our energy bodies and become initiated. We have to be our own priests and priestesses and form our own rituals.

Simplicity is the key-word which enables our rituals to be powerful but safe. Simple prayer, invocation and ceremonial will strengthen our links with the spiritual worlds, enable symbolic communion and strengthen our energy bodies. Rituals can be private, a matter for 'two or three gathered together' – usually as witnesses to some rite of passage or tie-cutting – or more public, as in celebrations.

The elements – earth, air, fire and water – should have a part in all rituals. You can have pot plants, feathers, lighted candles and a bowl of fresh water simply to honour and represent these elements. Alternatively you can bring substance to ritual by use of simple ceremonies such as planting seeds, invoking the breath of life, burning objects symbolic of that which is being left behind or purified, and scattering water for blessing or cleansing.

Meditation

Prayer, invocation and ritual can be aids to the achievement of the altered state of consciousness which is meditation (see also page 15). They might also be seen as forms of meditation themselves. The dictionary tells us that meditation is: 'the act of meditating; deep thought; serious continuous contemplation, especially on a religious or spiritual theme; a meditative discourse; a meditative treatment of a literary or musical theme'.

There is a similarity and interdependence between prayer, invocation, ritual and meditation. They give rise to each other and are major keys to the art of obtaining and following effective spiritual help and guidance.

GILDAS

In our world, it is as though we live in a river of light and colour. Angelic presences, our own energy bodies and the luminosity of all your higher selves reflect a dazzling intensity of light. In the countdown to the coming of the golden age on earth, you too will become more and more conscious of this stream of light and your ability to interact with it and have it interact with you. Any connections which you attempt, times you set aside, prayers or invocations in which you include reference to angels and guides helps to bring the stream of light consciousness ever more steadily into your hearts and minds and into the substance of the earth itself.

Within matter, there is also light and reflection. When the two streams truly meet and complement each other, then the changes in the substance of matter which are a part of the golden age will be enabled.

Angels, particularly archangels, may have seemed distant or inaccessible. Now they have become more conscious of the need to make bridges of light, directly into your hearts and lives. They want to facilitate an easier and daily connection with each one of you as individuals and not only to be available as part of legend, ceremonial or organised religion.

Speaking for the guides, we also seek a closer companionship and communion with you. We seek cooperation and friendship. We welcome your approaches to us and work towards the time when there can be easy dialogue between the planes and those who inhabit them. Your work and our work are one – we merely accomplish it from a different perspective and states of being.

We are not divine or godlike, but we see through a wider lens and from a different dimension than those you experience on the earth plane. We have a wider access to, and vision of, the jewel of truth. We are relieved of the problem of the burdens of the ego. We live in a consciousness of love and its transforming power. We are therefore more related to the divine principle and able to help you make your aspiration to connection with divine consciousness.

We can give you a hand along the way, ease your fears and open your minds to possibilities. We can help you to become accustomed to greater intensities of light, and so aid your journey to communion with high energies and the ability to honour the divine within yourselves. Invoke us as helpers, transformers, interpreters – never as beings of omniscience, omnipresence or omnipotence. Those attributes belong to the divine source of all life.

Exercises Relating to this Chapter

Guided Journey to the River of Light

(It is particularly important to read this meditation through before you do it. There are choices to be made during the journey, and you might like to meditate on or consider those choices before you begin.)

Sit or lie in a comfortable but symmetrically balanced position. Make sure that you will be undisturbed, that you have a blanket for warmth, and crayons, pencils and paper on hand for any recording you wish to do.
  Be aware of the rhythm of your breathing . . . gradually bring that rhythm into your heart centre or chakra . . . Travel on the heart energy into your inner landscape . . . Find yourself in the meadow . . . Awaken your inner senses, so that you see the objects and colours around you . . . hear the sounds . . . smell the fragrances . . . touch the textures . . . and taste the tastes . . . Ask for your inner wise presence to accompany you or to bless this journey, and make sure that you call to you any talisman or amulet you wish to take . . .
  From the meadow travel to the usual landing-stage where your main river boat is anchored . . . Ask your guardian angel and inner wise presence to help take you in the boat to the place on the river where you might best connect with the river of light . . . Settle yourself in the boat, content, on this occasion at least, to let others steer and power the vessel . . .
  You will travel upstream, towards the source . . . Be aware of the direction in which you are travelling and of the landscape through which you pass . . . Whenever you travel on the river make mental notes of areas

which you have not yet fully explored, but may wish to in the future . . .

Eventually the boat will come to a very still place on the river . . . It is almost like a self-contained pond, with reeds and flowers on the banks . . . trees reflected in the water and a clear view of mountains . . . You may recognise these mountains as those in which your river has its source . . . or if your source was on flatter ground . . . then these mountains lie beyond your source . . .

The light on the almost still waters of this place is brilliant and golden . . . You feel rested and at peace, and everything around you seems heightened in natural intensity and life-force . . . You may even see the life-force streaming from reeds, flowers and trees and shimmering in the golden light . . . As you look towards the mountains they seem to be joined to this place by a rainbow bridge of light and colour . . .

You long to travel across this bridge . . . and as the desire increases, your guardian angel surrounds you with its presence . . . It is as though you are held in angel's wings . . . Then you are travelling across the rainbow bridge together, whilst your inner wise presence guards your boat . . . For the next fifteen to twenty minutes the opportunity is yours . . . Through the mountains which lie beyond your source flows a river of light . . . or a network of interconnecting streams of light . . . Your guardian angel will take you wherever you ask and help you to meet whomsoever you would like to meet . . .

The choice is considerable and your own landscape will reveal its particular possibilities . . . but here are some suggestions . . . You may choose to . . .

Enter a natural sanctuary and meet with your true guide;

Journey to a crystal cave and receive healing;

Invoke the presence of an archangel, receive its blessing and bathe in its light;

Explore the network of streams of light and become particularly aware of the nature spirits at work and play;

Rest in a particularly lovely glade and ask your guardian angel to bring you guidance in a waking dream.

Your psyche will know when between fifteen to twenty minutes has passed, and your guardian angel will signify that it is time to return to the boat . . .

Once you have made an inner world journey you can repeat it, so have no regrets about the possibilities you missed in your exploration . . .

When you have been welcomed aboard your boat by your inner wise presence you will return to the landing-stage and thence to the meadow . . .

From the meadow you will return to the rhythm of your beathing in your heart centre . . . to awareness of the whole of your body and its connection with the ground . . . to your everyday surroundings and the opportunity to record your journey . . .

Put a cloak of light with a hood of light right around you before you return to your everyday tasks.

Reflection on Your Journey

With this journey there are no particular questions to ask. Just reflect on the possibilities your river of light holds, the choices you made this time and the choices you intend to make in the future with the help of this guided meditation.

Archangels

Prepare a set of cards with the names of the archangels
and their main attributes recorded on one side of them
(see pages 82–3). For example: MICHAEL – 'Who is like the
divine?', protector of the north, night, winter, the realms
of spirit and dreaming, guardian of peace, harmony and
global cooperation. Teaches us to ask the right question.

Turn the cards face downwards and let your intuition
lead you to the archangel who can most inspire and help
you at present.

Write an invocation to the archangel of your choice
and say it aloud three times in a strong voice. Before you
make the invocation, make sure that you are standing or
sitting in a well-balanced position. Have a sense of your
own space and your own 'ground'. Be aware of your
body. Breathe deeply and regularly.

Design a Ritual

If there is an event, celebration, new beginning, tie-
cutting or rite of passage which you would like to mark,
design a ritual. Enlist the help of your partner or some
friends, if appropriate.

Appreciating Your Guardian Angel

Take a large sheet of paper. Establish a quiet space
around you. Imagine your guardian angel standing
behind you, with wings spread in order to protect you.
Draw your impression of your guardian angel on your
piece of paper. At the bottom left-hand corner of your
completed drawing, write the word 'birth'. Then,
working round the edge of the drawing from left to
right, write down all the moments at which, in

retrospect, you realise your angel was with you to guard
you, protect you or soften the impact of the difficult
moments of your life.

Case History: The River of Life

Belinda came to me in a very confused state. The only
child of parents with very strong control mechanisms,
she had had a difficult childhood. When she went to
train as a nurse she was, at first, glad to be away from
the constrictions and the invasive atmosphere at home.
Yet the old patterns pulled her back and although, with
varying shifts and duties, it was easier for her to have a
room in the nurses' home, after a while she found herself
living with her parents again.

By the time she came to see me she had finished her
training and was working as a staff nurse on a medical
ward in a large teaching hospital.

The yo-yo pattern between home and independence
had continued. Returning to her parents was a compulsion, even though, when she was there, they treated her
like a child and she seemed powerless to stand up to
them.

Recently she had felt further confused when she began
to see colours and pictures around patients. Sometimes,
in the street, she would feel warm and see a light around
herself. At other times she would experience frightening
surges of blackness and feel surrounded by a fog of
depression. Belinda felt that life on earth was a burden
and was disproportionately sad and hopeless whenever
she observed any jealous, mean, greedy or controlling
behaviour in human interactions.

Obviously Belinda had become very sensitive in a
psychic sense. She was seeing auras and clairvoyant
pictures. She was being invaded by, and carrying,

darkness and fear from the collective bank of human emotions and experience. It was difficult for her to feel herself as a complete and separate being – a difficulty which had its origins at the psychological level. With such obsessively controlling parents, she had never really become a separate person. Her ego structure was very vulnerable.

Basic psychlogical work and tie-cutting on a relatively long-term basis were essential; but acknowledging her sensitivities, helping her to understand them and working at a spiritual level was also of great comfort. She learned simple exercises to strengthen her auric field (see opposite) and help her to be more in control of what she 'saw' and absorbed from those around her.

When, after the initial psychological and spiritual work, she made her journey to the river of light she was greatly strengthened and her sensitivities were confirmed by it. Contact with her guardian angel helped her to understand more of the pattern of her life until the present moment. Her favourite place on the river of light was a crystal sanctuary in which she found a special connection to the Archangel Gabriel, who became her great spiritual supporter.

Belinda identified her key-word for her life's purpose as 'healing'. So she is still nursing and finds fulfilment in her work. With her strong connection to Gabriel she is considering an eventual move into community nursing, or the possibility of training in social work. She has also done a healing course, and finds many opportunities to channel more subtle forms of healing to the patients in her care.

Belinda now has a small flat which is home to her. She visits her parents regularly without staying overnight and free of the old feeling of compulsion.

Basic Exercise for Strengthening and Protecting the Aura

Stand or sit with your feet firmly on the ground, your spine straight and your head well balanced on your neck. Visualise an egg of rose-pink light surrounding you. It goes over your head and under your feet. (Light interpenetrates with physical matter, so the floor is not a barrier to it.)

Beyond the egg of rose-pink light you are going to visualise seven more eggs of light. (The final effect is rather like those Russian dolls which fit one inside the other, with you at the centre.) The second egg of light (around and beyond the rose-pink egg) is amber; the third, golden yellow; the fourth, spring green; the fifth, clear, bright blue; the sixth, deep lapis lazuli blue; the seventh, violet; the eighth, silver.

Hold the vision of the eggs of light for about five minutes and then carry on with your normal everyday activities.

It is good to do this exercise each morning as you start your day, each evening before you sleep, and at any other time when you are facing a situation in which you know you may feel vulnerable.

6

Hidden Currents and Underground Streams

Something hidden. Go and find it. Go and look
   behind the Ranges –
Something lost behind the Ranges. Lost and
   waiting for you. Go.

RUDYARD KIPLING

*Aspects of love ... The masculine and feminine principle
... Creativity and sexuality ... Order and chaos ...
Abundance, letting go and holding on ...*

Aspects of Love

The word 'love' must be one of the most frequently used
– and misused – words in the English language. We love
our parents, each other, animals, colours, textures,
flavours, sports and weathers. We rarely love ourselves. Lack of vocabulary with which to describe
different shades of love and affection leads to
emotional confusion.

Within the accepted mores and conditioning of society
lies the assumption that parents will have a natural love
for their children, and children for their parents and
siblings. I see many clients experiencing deep distress or
guilt when love of, or for, family members fails to meet

these expectations. (Gildas comments from a spiritual perspective on page 114.)

We have already seen that parental love can be conditional. Family life also provides our main role models of male and female behaviour, and affects our capacity to embrace different aspects of love. Within the family we are imprinted with our attitudes to basic and mutual human respect, sexual and erotic, parental and filial, and to that spiritually embracing love which the Greeks called 'agape'. Deep undercurrents affect our lives when any, or all of these aspects of love is lacking, limited or eroded.

Romantic love

The Greek 'eros' gives us our word 'erotic'. The original meaning embraces tenderness and commitment as well as sexuality.

In the late eighteenth century the birth of the 'Romantic Era' gave us the archetypal pattern of 'romantic love', bringing expectations about relationships which are by no means all positive and which have affected us all. The heart has become the focus of love, passion and undying devotion. Eros has become Cupid, the god who creates chaos by firing darts of romance into defenceless and unsuspecting hearts. Particularly around St Valentine's Day, 14 February, the heart symbol appears everywhere.

The heart chakra is an important subtle energy centre, but notions of romantic love seriously impair our ability to develop it effectively and to understand its true spiritual significance. (See *Working with Your Chakras*, details of which can be found in the Bibliography.)

Romantic love has been hyped into big business. It is the theme of thousands of novels, short stories, films and television programmes. They almost invariably portray people who are helplessly in love, blind with passion, out of control of their emotions, and wreaking havoc on their own, and everybody else's, lives. Romantic love is possessive and selfish, gives rise to competition, creates jealousy, focuses on the body beautiful, derides the plain and homely, and stereotypes male and female roles.

The themes of romantic love stories are often shallow versions of myths and fairytales. The original myths and legends emerged from deep wisdom within each culture. Tales of knights in shining armour who slay dragons and rescue maidens, princes who cut their way through previously impassable thorns to awaken a sleeping beauty, and heroes searching the earth for the gift which is essential to winning the heroine's heart are all tales of wisdom. They give instruction in the development of life skills, the management of sexuality and the integration of the shadow. They often symbolise the journey of the soul.

Tales of romantic love harbour illusion. They encourage false expectations, foster depression and discontent, and perpetuate dangerous illusions. They fail to address the deeper issues of sexuality or to illustrate positive life skills. We are beguiled by this powerful archetype as well as conditioned by it.

A *sense* of romance, however, is highly desirable, and there is nothing wrong with those diversions which bring welcome but temporary escape and relaxation from the rigorous demands of day-to-day living. The danger arises when a disregard for spiritual values results in a high level of collusion between fictional trifles and destructive elements in our value system, which can completely colour our life conduct.

The Masculine and Feminine Principles

Our usually rich language fails us once more when it comes to naming the two fundamental principles of creation. By common usage, masculine belongs to men and feminine to women. Thus, when endeavouring to understand the masculine and feminine principles we become confused by issues which relate to expected, or stereotyped, male and female behaviours.

In her book *Knowing Woman*, Catherine Claremont de Castelliego defines the feminine principle as 'diffuse awareness' and the masculine, as 'focused attention'. These are useful definitions, but the Chinese words and symbols yin and yang enable even deeper insights to be acquired.

The Yin/Yang Symbol

Yin is dark, receptive, yielding, fecund, gestating, soft and diffuse, whilst yang is light, active, thrusting, fertile, propagating, hard and focused. Yin is the feminine principle and yang the masculine. In the diagram, the seed of yang is also within yin and the yin is in yang. Each circular seed is also a yin/yang diagram itself, showing that the interaction is constant into infinity.

The total diagram represents the principle of creation. It is important, particularly in understanding the function of light and dark in the principles, to let go of any conditioned reflexes which see dark as 'bad' and light as 'good', as well as any tendency to see yin as 'woman' and yang as 'man'. In this context, as when referring to electricity, dark is the negative polarity and light the positive. Dark is formless, like the negative of a photographic film. Light is differentiated and available to consciousness, like the positive of a photographic film.

Whether we are male or female, we make use of both principles all day and every day in our phsyical, mental, emotional and spiritual lives. Certainly, at the physical level, men will have an advantage in performing active, thrusting tasks whilst women are more at home when providing receptivity and softness – but these are variables, not absolutes. Our society often labels men who have easy access to the feminine principle as 'sissy', whilst women with drive and brainpower may be seen as 'wearing the trousers' or 'pushy'. The role of man and woman is closest to a match of principle with gender in the basic, heterosexual act of sexual intercourse.

The yin/yang diagram shows the 'eye' or 'seed' of each principle as being included and intrinsic within the other. Even if women have easier access to the feminine principle and men to the masculine, part of the inner spiritual journey which leads us to fuller understanding of the creative principles involves learning to relate to, and respecting, the masculine or feminine within.

Jung taught about the anima in man and the animus in woman. These are our internal, invisible partners who lead us away from the effects of conditioning and stereotyping of gender to a happy inner balance. The more we are on terms with the seed of the opposite gender within, the more we can live balanced and creative lives and have a fuller understanding of these basic principles of creation. Befriending the animus or anima also helps us to create relationships with the opposite sex which are open, honest, mature and free from idealistic projections and expectations, and in which we escape the possessiveness and illusion of romantic love. In many spiritual matters there are paradoxes. Relationships in which both partners have come to terms with their animus and anima often come full circle. When free of the pitfalls and illusions of romantic love, there is often a greater freedom to act romantically.

Creativity and Sexuality

The capacity to be creative means far more than being able to make lovely things or to produce works of art. Creativity includes creative ideas and originality. Being spiritually creative means having the ability to live harmoniously even when 'the chips are down'.

Creativity occurs when two known factors combine to yield something new. Inextricably linked to the interaction of the masculine and feminine principles, it is enacted in the fundamental sexual act of procreation.

There are many factors which can block our creativity. Its rudimentary root lies in sexuality and procreation. Any sexual 'hang-ups', difficulties with sexual identity or over-riding moral and judgemental attitudes to sexual expression all limit our ability to have a fully creative approach to life. Issues of power, or lack of 'permission' to be ourselves or to be completely adult, may mean that full creativity lies dormant or surrounded with pain and frustration as it struggles for birth.

In chakra terms, most of these issues are connected with the sacral chakra whose element is water. When the river flows smoothly, problems do not accumulate; but where there are hidden currents, eddies, whirlpools and underground streams, clearance may be essential. Working directly with the sacral chakra aids the accomplishment of such clearance.

Frustrated creativity often emerges as anger. One way of dealing with anger is to find some constructive or imaginative outlet for its energy. If this is not possible, violence, which is the shadow side of creativity, may erupt. The creative urge is primal. When it is thwarted it becomes counter-productive, causing destruction, tyranny and – the ultimate abuse of the life-force – destruction of life itself.

Working to find a balance of the masculine and feminine within helps us to be integrally creative and to take full responsibility for that which we cause to come into being. Our collective inventions have produced the toxins which threaten our lives and the life of our planet. We are now being forced to take note, to revise our behaviour and to use our creative abilities in other directions than the manipulation of the earth's resources to satisfy our greed.

One of the most dangerous theories of recent years suggests that the condition in which we find ourselves, and the prevalence of diseases such as AIDS, are the result of a divine curse. We have misbehaved and are being punished. When we become obedient and docile once more, we shall be forgiven. God will end our punishment, remove the curse and decree that harmony should flow once more.

This theory evades responsibility, denies the divine within each one of us, and cuts us off from the possibility of co-creatorship.

Co-Creatorship

Many of our collective creations have proved to be autonomous monsters. When we take full responsibility for what we have done we will be able to contact the divine spark within and find antidotes and solutions which are more in tune with the sacred pattern of the universe. Once we are truly in harmony with the gift of creativity, we will have reached the stage of enabling the birth of a truly golden age. This cannot be created *for* us, only *with* us, as fully conscious and participant co-creators.

Chaos and Order

We fear chaos and seek order. Yet too much control or regimentation denies individuality and freedom, stifles inspiration and destroys creativity.

Chaos and order appear to be polarities. We experience them as opposite ends of a scale. We have a tendency to assume that one side of a polarity represents weakness or the undesirable, whilst the other represents strength and advantage. Polarities play a major part in our conditioning.

In fact, the more polarised two factors are, the more corrosive each can become. Jung spoke of 'the transcendent principle', which is reached when opposites are contemplated from a point above, and between them (see diagram on page 110). From this angle of perception a point of balance can be reached. The confusion and divided loyalties which result from polarisation cease, and the essential interdependence of opposites is understood.

The Transcendent Principle

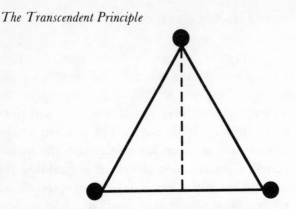

The minute observation made possible by the sophisticated instruments of modern science has enabled the energy patterns of order and chaos to be tracked and recorded, with the result that chaos can no longer be categorised as a destructive force. The patterns of order are limited, circumscribed and repetitive. The patterns of chaos may at first seem disorganised, but lead to new and exciting possibilities.

In speaking of the nature of breakdown and change, Gildas has often said that life is like a mosaic. When the known pattern breaks apart we become very frightened and fragmented – yet it may be that very fragmentation which enables us to rearrange the component parts in such a way that a new, more pleasing and harmonious pattern is formed. In the process, unwanted or outworn components can be discarded and new possibilities included.

Chaos not only shatters the mosaic so that it can be rearranged, it opens up the old pattern so that new discoveries may take place. Chaos resolves itself into a new order and is essential to creativity and the progression of knowledge. Our attitudes to chaos have to be redefined.

Abundance, Letting Go and Holding On

Nature is both prolific and prodigal. Abundance is all about us. As human beings we have learned to stockpile and to use possessions as a measure of self-esteem and importance. We have become possessed by the negative archetype of greed. We are betrayed by a lack of trust in nature and ourselves. We have exploited the earth's resources, and fear that nature will rebound upon us. We have become panicked by the concept that 'time is running out'. We are creating our own brand of chaos. Yet if the energies which have been recorded run true to form, out of that chaos will come a new order.

This thought should not make us complacent or reckless. We must not let go in the wrong way. It is always less painful when we can go with the flow, but we should not do so as a piece of flotsam or jetsam. Going with the flow means observing the currents and tides and using them to empower us. The surfer can ride the waves skilfully, but cannot make them happen – and, ultimately, is dependent on the pattern of the wave itself.

We cannot interfere with the basic and sacred design of the universe, but we can learn to use resources and energies skilfully and respectfully. What is true of our relationship to the greater universe is true of our personal, intimate and immediate universes. We are the microcosm within the macrocosm. Through personal management we learn wider management. Making the most of individual resources and pursuing self-knowledge without becoming narcissistic is the greatest contribution which we can make to the evolution of the whole.

Because we fear chaos and elevate order we want to

hold on to the known, thinking in this way to ensure security. In so doing we may fail to recognise that some of our so-called securities have become negative self-fulfiling prophecies. Greed generates scarcity. Stockpiling results in decay and devaluation.

At the psychological level we often pay a high price for what we regard as security. Negative beliefs about ourselves and our potential cause negative actions and reaction, which in turn reinforce or justify the original belief. This is the mechanism of self-fulfilling prophecy. We create our own worlds, but are infinitely more experienced at creating them destructively rather than constructively.

It takes energy to hold on to things. When we let go we may suffer a sense of loss, but this loss is often quickly followed by a sense of freedom and an upsurge of vitality.

'Let go and let God' is a well-worn and over-simplistic cliché, but there is an underlying truth within it which we do well to contemplate from time to time. Letting go consciously is a far different prospect from having things wrenched out of our unwilling arms. With the wonders of modern science to demonstrate to us that letting go leads to unforeseen beauty, our excuses for holding on lessen daily. The value of trust is being proven.

Here are Gildas's words on some of these issues.

GILDAS

Within the pattern of individual evolution certain lives are 'key lives'. In these lifetimes you carry an extra consciousness which is linked to personal authority, responsibility and co-creatorship. If you are reading these words it is likely that you have become aware of your spiritual needs and are consciously seeking spiritual growth.

Such a desire indicates an evolutionary awakening – or a key life. Whatever you live and assimilate in such a lifetime is not merely added to the sum total of your incarnate journeys, but enables your soul more thoroughly to integrate all its learning. A key life registers as a beam of light on the soul thread [see *A Message of Love*, detailed in the Bibliography] so that past and future experiences are clearly seen and brought into context as a meaningful progression.

You live in times when you have to take a great deal of responsibility for your desire to grow. You must search ardently to find answers. You have to cultivate your own inner authority, which may entail considerable clearance work to enable the river of life to flow cleanly, clearly and without obstruction. Inevitably, in the course of such clearance, you will be confronted and challenged by the issue of love and its many facets. Part of the challenge at the spiritual level is that spiritual and social law do not always coincide. Socially you are expected to love your parents.

Spiritually it can be recognised that some parents are genetic parents only. Children can be of quite a different 'substance' from their parents and siblings, and can come from a different soul group or spiritual family. As life progresses, the true spiritual family is usually found. Once clearance of difficult psychological material has been made, even though parents may be recognised as genetic parents and not of true spiritual family, it should still be possible to respect them, or have compassion for them as fellow human beings on their own journey of evolution.

No spiritual law obliges you to love your genetic family other than in this way. All fellow human beings should be honoured, but you are not an unforgivable traitor if you love friends and peers more than your family of birth.

Love is important on all levels of being but, whilst incarnate, knowing that you are loved can lessen the feeling of being an exile. Love and acceptance go hand in hand, and it is hard for you to function well on earth if you feel judged, misunderstood or ostracised. It is difficult for you to 'get right' with the divine or the spiritual, unless you first feel right with parents, siblings, peers and partners.

Accepting that human love is fallible and not always available in the quality you long for is a challenging truth to learn. Even more challenging may be the realisation that you have failed to give quality love to others, because some obstacle has interrupted the smooth flow of the stream.

Yet take heart, for your expectations show that this quality of love does, in fact, exist. The experience you seek, yet also fear to trust, is all around you. The basic pattern of the universe is a pattern of love. When you cease to fear, when you let go, instead of holding on you will enter the love stream in full consciousness and all barriers will fall.

Whatever obstacles your inner psychological experiences and messages have produced, practise feeling loved. Do not attach this feeling or expectation to any other being. Seek only to take in, on each in-breath, an enfolding, unconditional love from the cosmic source. In letting the energy in you will awaken your unconditional love centre, and will also begin to breathe the same pure energy out. Thus love in the universe will intensify. Gradually all will be touched and healed by its flow, so that the true potential for collective humanity can unfold.

The understanding and balancing of the masculine and feminine principles becomes ever more crucial as human evolution reaches the point where the golden age becomes possible. Through this balance creative potential will be enhanced, enabling a very important step in evolution to be taken.

Relationships of all kinds will mature as never before in the history of humankind. When any individual ceases to look to others to provide the counter-balance for that which is lacking in him/herself, then a healthy self-sufficiency is reached. A partnership, or group of two or more such persons, means that the possibilities and permutations of creativity are vastly increased.

At previous spiritual turning-points the complementary relationship between priest and priestess has been the pivotal point of balance. Now, the possibility of something much more sophisticated is emerging. Greater responsible freedom of sexual expression, and valuing, rather than condemning or merely 'giving permission' for homosexual relationships, also play a significant part in these revelations.

A great deal of the difficulty of your present incarnate exposure is attributable to the increasing presence of chaotic factors. Old orders have to break down if advances are to be made. If progress is to be more than a reorganisation of the old, then chaos must positively be embraced in order to bring new possibilities to birth. Chaos is a form of random selection where all factors present will not previously have been known or experienced. It takes courage to welcome chaos as a friend and healer, but these it can become when fear of change drops away.

Try not to fear letting go of the old order. That which is worthy will survive to become a part of the new, and only the dross will fall definitively away. Chaos is a divine principle, not a threatening invader.

Exercises Relating to this Chapter

Guided Journey to Reviewing the Hidden Currents and Underground Streams of the River of Life

Sit or lie in a comfortable, but symmetrically balanced position, making sure that you will be undisturbed. Have ready a blanket for warmth, and crayons and paper for any recording you wish to do.

Be aware of the rhythm of your breathing . . . gradually bring that rhythm into your heart centre or chakra . . . Travel on the heart energy into your inner landscape . . . Find yourself in the meadow . . . Awaken your inner senses, so that you see the objects and colours around you . . . hear the sounds . . . smell the fragrances . . . touch the textures . . . and taste the tastes . . . Ask your inner wise presence to accompany you, or to bless this journey . . . Make sure that you have any talisman or amulet you wish to take . . .

On this occasion you will not travel by boat, but will choose a colour on which to traverse your landscape in order to get a fresh overview of the river of your life . . . As you look around your meadow, you see that there is a rainbow which has its beginning here . . . The translucent colour streams are flowing to earth in such a way that you can go and stand in their midst and bathe in their hues . . . As you bathe in light and colour, you receive any healing you need and feel your vitality being recharged . . .

Choose one of these rainbow colours on which to travel . . . Let it wrap itself around you until you are so full of its light that you can travel effortlessly wherever you will . . .

Travel, on the light colour of your choice, from the meadow to the river of your life . . . Move wherever you wish, over and above the river and landscape . . . As you do so, take a fresh overview of the course of your river . . .

From this angle, and with the aid of the light on which you travel, you will become particularly aware of any unusual currents . . . whirlpools . . . eddies, obstacles or dams in the natural flow . . . You are acquiring a view of your river which is different from anything you have noticed on your previous voyages . . .

Choose a feature of which you are now aware, to observe more closely . . . Using the light on which you travel, come as close to this feature as you wish . . . Let the light illuminate this aspect of your river, showing its interaction with the main stream as clearly as possible . . . As you look, ask that the coloured light may also illuminate or awaken any memories or insights about the influences in your life which have caused this irregularity in your river . . . Are there difficulties or blockages which you encounter time and time again, preventing you from entering the mainstream of your potential? . . . Are you symbolically trapped in a whirlpool? . . . Pulled along too fast or impeded by a current? . . . Is there flotsam or jetsam causing blockages or diversions in the natural flow of your creative or sexual energy? . . .

Spend five minutes contemplating the obstacle of your

choice and, with the help of your coloured light, seeking
insight as to the underlying causes which have brought
it into being, and what it represents in your life . . .
Call upon your guardian angel to give you support and
to shed its light, also into this process of
illumination . . .

Not all the currents, whirlpools or diverted flows will
be negative . . . Some hidden currents may represent
neglected and undeveloped talents or aspects of yourself
which you have been prevented from focusing on or
cultivating . . . Using your light, and accompanied by
your guardian angel, explore a further hidden aspect
of your river's flow and ask for any hidden gifts, talents
or unexpected resources to be illuminated . . . Again,
take five minutes to allow insights to develop . . .

Beneath the river bed itself, an underground stream
may flow . . . If so, somewhere along the course of your
river there will be an entrance to it via a rocky place,
hollow or cavern . . . Continuing to travel on your
coloured light, search for any evidence of an opening to
an underground stream . . . If you find such a place,
land lightly and gently near the opening . . . With the
aid of your light and colour, and supported by your
guardian angel and your inner wise presence, look in at
the stream . . . Allow it to be illuminated, without going
further to explore it . . .

Recognise that casting this light into the underground
stream may be the trigger or catalyst which enables
deeper insights into the course and purpose of your life
to emerge in their own time . . . These insights may be
about other lifetimes . . . They may show how your
uppermost consciousness is so absorbed in the main flow
of the river that you neglect your inner life . . . forget, or
do not listen to, your dreams . . . have insights and plans
for your life which somehow never come to fruition . . .

fear to let go of the mainstream in order to take risks –
even calculated ones.

If you have found the entrance to an underground
stream, let the light shine into its flow for five minutes as
you contemplate its energy and meanings . . .

When you are ready, travel on your coloured light
stream back to the rainbow in your meadow . . . thank
your inner wise presence and your guardian angel for
their support . . . Leave the rainbow and come into the
familiar meadow . . .

From the meadow, return to your awareness of your
breath in your heart centre . . . Gradually return to your
normal surroundings . . . Feel your contact with the
ground . . . Visualise the symbol of a cross of light in a
circle of light over your heart chakra, as a blessing.

Take time to reflect on your journey and to make
notes and drawings in your river of life workbook.

Reflections on Your Journey

Many reflections this time are actually built into the
journey. Some of the themes which have presented
themselves here may have appeared before. This journey
gives you the opportunity to meet them from a different
perspective and review them at a deeper level.

The following are mainly repetitions of the questions
which were put during the journey, with some additions.

On which colour did you choose to travel?
Make your own associations to the significance of this
colour, before reading the notes on colour in the
Glossary.

Do you easily neglect your inner life?
If you are following the exercises in this book you are

probably trying to rectify this neglect, but time for
yourself, respect for your thoughts and aspirations and
inner musings, visiting your inner landscape and time
just to 'be' are important factors in spiritual growth.

Do you record and listen to your dreams?
Even if you find it difficult to remember your dreams,
recording fragments, or the images and feelings which
come just before going to sleep or immediately on
waking, will signal to your psyche that you want to
listen to its more secret life. Do not struggle to analyse
your dreams. Keep a dream book, and read through it
from time to time. Gradually, any important messages
that your dreams have for you will become clear.

*Are there insights you have had about your life, or plans you have
made, which you have never implemented?*
Re-consider these now, reviewing the reasons which
prevent you from putting certain things into action. Are
there insurmountable practical considerations? Are you
reluctant to embrace change?

If you have tended to hang back, do not put yourself
under pressure and criticism or feel guilty. Our dreams
and aspirations cannot always be brought to fruition.
Sometimes we have to accept the status quo, and grow
spiritually by learning to live with it gracefully. But in
this review, see if there are any real regrets or any
positive and creative actions you can resolve to take.

Are you afraid to take risks – even calculated ones?
As with the previous question, if your answer is in the
affirmative do not become self-condemnatory. Merely
reflect on the factors in your life which have made risk-
taking seem so dangerous. Consider whether you would
like to make changes in your attitudes. How could you

help yourself to a greater basic security, in order to be less wary of risks? Do you need to look again at the section on the inner child (page 57)?

Do you take too many risks?
Are you searching too ardently? Are you looking thoroughly at the landscape through which you travel, and really seeing what it has to offer? Or are you racing ahead, to see what is around the next corner, without reading the signs and signals? Are you happy with a fast pace? Do you want or need to slow down?

Did you see neglected or unexpected talents?
How could you use or develop them, even in small ways?

Was there flotsam and jetsam in your river?
If so, try to see what this may symbolise, and how the energy it is blocking may be released. As suggested in the visualisation, the flow which is impeded may be connected with creative or sexual energies. Review the messages you got from your parents about love and sexuality. How was, and is, the sexual 'climate' of your life? What healing do you need? Go back to this part of your river and invoke help to transform or remove the blockages. (see Chapter 5). Are there still ties which need to be cut (see page 64)?

Is some aspect of your life trapped in a whirlpool?
Which problem areas of your life tend to recur over and over again? Do you keep going over old ground? Reflect on how you could get free from the whirlpool, and how you might put up markers on your river to warn of its existence and dangers.

There may be a positive aspect to the whirlpool, in

that sometimes we need to go over similar ground but at a different level of the spiral. Some problems can only be tackled layer by layer. Some whirlpools disappear if we can gradually go deep enough into them to find the source of their current.

The Masculine and Feminine Principle

1. Make a list of those tasks in your life which require more masculine principles and those which require more feminine. If there is an imbalance (taking into account whether you are a man or a woman), try to see how you could 'befriend' the other principle and make greater use of it.

2. Make a list of the life activities which you tend to associate with women and those you associate with men. Are there certain tasks which you feel women 'should' be good at? Tasks which men 'should' automatically take on, or excel in? (Be honest!) What do these reflections tell you about your gender role models and conditioning?

3. Meditate on the yin/yang diagram on page 105.

Love

1. Consider the different kinds of love you have known in your life. Which aspects of love flow most easily for you? How could you use these strengths to help more love flow into your life and to help you be more conscious of the love you give in life?

2. Do Gildas's exercise on page 114.

Letting Go and Holding On

Review the times in your life when you have had to
let go of something. Did you manage to do so
sufficiently to leave space for something positive and
new to come in? Do you still look back with regret?
Would cutting some ties help you to heal the wounds
and release energy into your life and future (see page 64)?

Chaos and Order

Think of any pair of opposites in your life which make
you feel ambivalent or divide your loyalties.
   Look at the diagram on page 110. Get an image for
each polarity. See them at opposite ends of a line. Invoke
your inner wise presence and/or guardian angel. Rise to
the point above and between the opposites. Seek a
symbol for the balance of the polarities.

Repeat the Guided Journey

When you are ready for more insights repeat this
journey, choosing a different colour on which to travel
and different currents and obstacles to explore.

Case History: Hidden Currents and Underground Streams

Frederick came for help because his wife, Sarah, had told
him he was becoming boring. She accused him of being
unexciting in his approach to work, leisure and in bed. She
had admitted that in many other ways he was a model
husband – but that, it seemed, was no longer enough.
   The marriage was a second one for both of them and
they had been together for five years. Basically, the

relationship was good and they had been happy. Soon after they married, Sarah had begun to attend transpersonal workshops. Working on herself had made her realise that she wanted to make changes in her life and attitudes. Frederick had not attended the workshops and was beginning to feel bewildered.

They both worked as architects. Sarah had two grown-up children from a previous marriage. During her child-rearing years she had done freelance work, which had gradually built up into a small business. Frederick had a 'safe' job with a local authority and was becoming increasingly frustrated with financial cuts. He did not know how to implement change without losing security.

One of the things which had first attracted Sarah to Frederick was the security he could offer. Now, she seemed to be irritated by it. She wanted some adventure and risk-taking in their lives before it became too late.

Sarah had succeeded in making Frederick feel restless. He realised that his heart must be in any changes made and that creative compromises would have to be found, but he was beginning to see that new horizons could do more than save his marriage. His main problem was fear of insecurity. An only child, born when his very conventional parents were in their forties, he felt he had never been a risk-taker.

When Frederick took the guided journey to find hidden currents and obstacles in his river, he encountered a great log-jam. Timber had been cut and was being floated downstream. The logs had been unattended and had got stuck in a narrowing part of the river, where they were almost blocking the flow by causing a dam.

Frederick's associations with this imagery were connected with an ambition he had had, when he was about fifteen years old, to go to Canada and become a lumberjack. He was very surprised to get in touch with this almost forgotten part of himself. He had really wanted to go and do something very physical, live a 'tough' life and take considerable risks. Frederick's parents had persuaded him that this was a 'storybook' dream. They had allowed him to go on an Outward Bound course, but refused to discuss or research any possibilities for the Canadian ambition to become a reality.

Frederick's mother had been very hurt by his desire to leave, and Frederick could not face her tears and grief whenever the subject was mentioned. He focused on his school work, and eventually felt that he was fulfilling his talents by studying architecture. He had always looked after his parents financially and practically until they had died, within six months of each other, just before he married Sarah.

Frederick had had a long courtship with a friend from his schooldays. Their eventual marriage had lasted only two years before, tragically, his wife died of leukaemia. Frederick had assuaged his grief by becoming more and more assiduous about caring for his parents. He had not gone back to his old home to live when his wife died, but had spent a great deal of time in parental involvement. He married Sarah ten years after his first wife died.

There was a great deal of unacknowledged loss and grief for Frederick to face. As the full picture emerged, Sarah was very supportive. She felt guilty about her earlier accusations, but Frederick saw them as a powerful catalyst which was enabling change.

Eventually Frederick applied for early retirement. He and Sarah had decided to offer their talents to the third world – an adventure which was a real creative compromise, satisfying each of them in different ways. The last time I saw Frederick he was happy and excited and on the verge of departure. Smiling rather diffidently, he said that Sarah no longer found him boring – in any way.

7

The Estuary and the Sea Beyond

A livelier emerald twinkles in the grass,
A purer sapphire melts into the sea.
ALFRED LORD TENNYSON

The wounded healer ... Elemental and spiritual fire ...
Transformation ... Death and rebirth ... Life as a ritual
dance ...

The Wounded Healer

Studying your astrological birth chart is an informative
and supportive means of mapping your spiritual journey.
At present there are twelve known signs of the zodiac:
Aries, Taurus, Gemini, Cancer, Leo, Virgo, Libra, Scor-
pio, Saggitarius, Capricorn, Aquarius and Pisces. Each
sign rules a part of the year, and our date of birth
determines our 'sun sign'. Most popular magazines and
newspapers carry daily or weekly predictions telling how
the changing positions of planets and stars are affecting
life for those born under each sign.

Such analyses, are, of course, too broad and general-
ised. This is because our birth charts are immensely
complex. There are very precise planetary interactions at
work at the moment at which we draw our first breath.

The individual birth chart, calculated by an astrologer, takes into account the exact time and place at which we are born. Skilled interpretation of the chart and its 'progressions' can be enormously hepful to a fuller understanding of ourselves and our life paths.

Each planet follows a precise but different course in the universe and in relationship to our own planet, earth. Each of the signs and each of the planets has a name, and these are linked to the great myths and archetypes. Studying the myths and archetypes helps us to understand these cosmic influences and our personal, as well as collective, interaction with them.

As humanity has evolved, so more planets have been 'discovered'. The ancients knew Saturn, Mercury, Jupiter, Mars, Venus, the Sun and the Moon. Later discoveries were Neptune, Pluto and Uranus. Astronomers, as well as astrologers, continually study the stars and planets. As more sophisticated equipment enables our vision to expand, new discoveries are made. The most recent, in 1977, is a planetoid which has been named Chiron (although even as I write this there is news of the sighting of a 'new' constellation, which would give a thirteenth sign to the zodiac.)

It is interesting to reflect what 'discovery' of an influence which has always been there, in the universe, means to our collective evolution, awareness and learning. In her book *Chiron and the Healing Journey* Melanie Reinhart says:

> The discovery of a new outer planet is a momentous event, suggesting that an archetypal pattern, another facet of the divine is being activated within the collective psyche, stirring below in the unconscious depths and seeking recognition. Jung believed that the human consciousness was indispensable for

the fulfilment of Creation, and in this sense we are all co-creators of the process of being and becoming, just as we are all created by the process. When a new planet is discovered, many synchronous events occur which express its archetypal theme; a distinct cluster of images and mythic figures can be seen at work within historical and political events and general trends within the collective, the meaning of which may also have enormous impact upon the individual psyche.

As the discovery and naming of the planetoid Chiron took place so comparatively recently, its symbolic message for us is particularly pertinent. In mythology, Chiron is a centaur – half horse and half man. When his mother, Philyra, saw her son, she felt she had given birth to a monster and asked the gods to change her into something other than she was. Thus, abandoning Chiron, she was turned into a lime tree. Apollo became Chiron's foster-father.

Chiron eventually became a teacher of healing and the skills of war, his most famous pupil being Asclepius, who brought healing to humankind.

Yet Chiron, accidentally wounded by one of Hercules's arrows, was unable to heal himself. Wounds from the arrows of Hercules were known to be incurable. Chiron was an immortal and he faced the fate of living throughout eternity, disabled and in pain from his wound. He has thus become known as 'the wounded healer'.

Chiron solved his dilemma by being allowed to bestow his immortality on Prometheus and become mortal himself. Prometheus had been condemned to eternal punishment for stealing the secret of fire from the gods. As an immortal, he was free to bestow fire as a gift to humanity and could thus be released from punishment. As a mortal,

Chiron could die of his wound and end his suffering. In compassion for his plight, Jupiter placed him as a star/planetoid in the constellation of Saggitarius.

There are many things to consider in the symbology of Chiron's life. He was abandoned by his mother, and never recognised by Cronos, his real father; he was half horse, half man; he became a teacher of healing and war; he carried an intolerable wound; he enabled fire to be a free gift to humanity, rather than a begrudged and punishable theft; and he found a creative solution to his own wounding.

Parental abandonment strikes deep chords for individuals, for society and for religion. The orphan must struggle for recognition, expends much energy seeking parenting, but nevertheless often undertakes the heroic journey (see Carol Pearson's *The Hero Within*, details of which can be found in the Bibliography). We live in a society where the 'family', including the welfare state, is breaking down. Most organised religions have given us a negative image of the divine as a parent. The difficult times in which we live give rise to the plaintive cry: 'Is God dead?' The escalating effects of our misuse of the earth make us fear that perhaps the great earth mother herself will deny us sustenance and throw us off the planet.

Philyra abandoned her son because he was half horse, half man. Yet this combination can symbolise a connection between instinct and intellect − a bridge that we certainly need to strengthen and rebuild. When we disregard our instincts we fail to observe natural rhythms and lose touch, at a very basic level, with any sense of meaning and purpose.

Perhaps because so much went wrong at the beginning of his life, Chiron achieved a high level of consciousness as he sought to heal himself. He was certainly well respected by the gods and became an expert in the skills of healing and war. We may question whether war is a

skill. When it is reactionary and motivated by untem-
pered anger, of course it is not; but if the warrior is seen
more symbolically, then great skills on all levels may be
required. Protection of boundaries and provision for peo-
ples are spiritual as well as mundane concerns. Our
voyage to discovering our true selves can be eroded
when our personal boundaries and self-respect are in a
weakened condition. We need the archetype of the wise
warrior to help us assert our true rights.

The setback of the accidental wounding by Hercules's
arrow must have been great indeed for Chiron. Pain and
disablement made it impossible for him to sustain a
fulfilling role. Wounded at the beginning of life, he must
now sustain a re-wounding which would be with him for
eternity – or find a creative solution. In choosing mortal-
ity, Chiron shows us that death itself can be healing. He
also teaches us that old wounds must be allowed to die
and that we should be wary of the re-wounding process.

We might ask how one who was so wounded could be
such a wise teacher of healers. A lot of despair can be
experienced when we realise the extent of our personal
and collective wounds. How can we heal ourselves and
each other if wounding is so universal? The spiritual
paradox, and the one which Chiron demonstrates, is that
in healing our own wounds we heal each other and the
earth. In learning to heal from the place of wounding we
are better able to invoke the healing required. We heal
from a place of whole understanding, rather than from a
place of perfection.

Elemental and Spiritual Fire

The gods were angry that fire had been stolen and given
to humans. Mastery of fire was something which set the

gods apart and which they guarded jealously. Chiron's solution to his own dilemma ensured that fire was given freely to earth and humanity, as a blessing.

The element of fire enables much more than heat, light, protection and a means of cooking. It is essential to the flow of the life-force itself. It is a means of transformation, enabling things to be tempered, moulded, changed and cleansed. Out of control, it is a great destroyer, but can remind us not to over-depend on old structures.

Emotionally, fire is a great motivator and makes us warm-hearted and passionate. Equally it can make us destructive, aggressive or violent. In learning to manage and contain the fire element, on every level, we learn balance and appropriate control.

The concept that we carry a spark of the divine within us is common to most spiritual and religious teachings. The bestowal of fire as a gift from the gods enables us to live spiritually and to recognise the spirit in matter. Each one of us has a pure spiritual flame within. When we succeed in relating to its quality in ourselves and each other, then all differences can be resolved and mutual respect becomes the order of the day.

Transformation

The spiritual voyage is one of transformation. Letting light into the dark side of experience so that it can fall away is a transformative process. Seeking the symbolic meaning of life transforms deeply wounding or confusing events and reveals their significance in the overall tapestry of life. That which cannot be cured must be healed by transformation.

Death and Rebirth

As transformation for his own suffering, Chiron chose a death which had creative repercussions. He realised that 'quality of life' could be more precious than life itself. For mortals, death is inevitable, though it often seems that the medical profession see it as a failure – both ours and theirs. Life without quality is often prolonged, whilst more cutting, poisoning and burning of the body are offered as 'treatment'. When faced with death we are often encouraged to hold on, instead of being helped and supported whilst we let go with dignity.

Most people, when asked, say that they do not fear death itself so much as the process of dying. This surely is an indicator that we drastically need to revise our attitudes to terminal care. There is movement in the right direction, but, sadly, there is little education about death and dying. Care which emphasises quality of life and quality of death still tends to be the privilege of the few. It will remain so until it is more acceptable to talk about death and to face its reality.

During life we have many 'little deaths' or rites of passage, often followed by rebirth. Puberty is the death of childhood but the birth of the sexually mature adult. Marriage, or committed partnership, is the death of youth and a certain freedom from responsibility, but the doorway to new horizons and experiences. Divorce, separation, loss of a job, retirement and chronic illness are all degrees of death, involving grief and loss, but when they are faced openly, surprising rebirths happen. Human beings have a capacity to bounce back and find hidden benefits in the most difficult situations.

Learning to handle the 'little deaths' helps us to prepare for the seeming finality of the death of the body and personality. If we have faced change consciously, we learn to honour grief and yet not be destroyed by it.

What we believe about death will affect our attitude to it. We have no objective proof of the afterlife or the continuance of being, yet there is a growing body of people who channel discarnate guides or beings who live in another dimension; those who have had near death experiences often speak of a reluctance to return from the light and love they have felt. It is interesting that, as such events are compared and a body of subjective evidence is gathered, some scientific researchers are at pains to put it all down to oxygen deprivation. We are often reluctant to accept that things need not be 'either/or' but can rather be 'and/and'.

Now Gildas wishes to speak about life and death as a ritual dance.

GILDAS

Within a dance, there are ritual movements. The dancers step forward and back, turn full circle, weave in and out, meet each other, dance together and pass on. One section of dancers will hold the boundaries whilst others perform intricate steps. Places will be changed, space given and taken, patterns formed, broken and re-formed. Rhythms pulsate, and all dancers harmonise, so that the dance may have its life and being.

Within the dance many lessons about life and death, holding on and letting go, order and chaos are symbolised. A bridge is made between earth and spirit. Even when it is not being danced, the dance, as a form, exists.

Dancing, even when energetic and exciting, is a graceful mode. By looking to the dance you can learn to live more gracefully, dance together more harmoniously and creatively allow the dance to die, knowing that it lives on.

Not only incarnate life is illustrated within the dance, but death, rebirth and reincarnation too. From the perspective of incarnation, death is a stepping back, whilst the others dance on. Yet as you step into death you join another dance, or series of dances, until eventually you feel ready to step back into the dance of incarnation once more.

As you progress into the golden age, the great series of dances, one contained within the other, will continue. You will live earth life in optimum health, knowing, as with the rhythm of the dance, when it is time to step back, when to step into another circle and when to return. Leaving one circle to dance in another will all be part of the greater web, and you will know that all who dance similar rhythms will meet again. Grief and loneliness will no longer be part of incarnate experience. Within these patterns, when change is required, the dance of chaos will be danced in consciousness, since its sacred rhythms will no longer be feared.

The 'golden age' is not a time of stasis. The dances and the dancers weave on and on, for perfection, or the exploration of wholeness, has many permutations and also contains the seeds of growth.

Try not to fear death. Your fears of transition are often based on being judged or clearly seen. The only judgement you will meet is that of love, which seeks only to discover the wounds which require healing and the imbalances which need creative rebalancing. When you are most clearly seen, you are most clearly understood, your deepest wounds are revealed and true healing can begin. When you think about death, think about love. When you think about reviewing the life you have lived, do not think about blame, shame, guilt or recrimination, but about being healed and learning how to heal others whom you may have wounded.

A lesson in the story of Chiron, which has not been spoken of, is that of his *accidental* wound by an arrow from Hercules's bow. It was not premeditated or intended – Chiron and Hercules were friends. A certain interaction of life-force and movement caused the wound to happen. No doubt Hercules learned much about the power of his arrows and the need therefore to be ever more conscious and responsible for their direction. Yet without that arrow and that wound, many creative opportunities would have been missed. The catalyst which causes change is not always comfortable. Being the catalyst, especially when the action is not deliberate, can be heartrending at the human level. From beyond death other perspectives are seen, and the process of maturity is very clearly understood.

These are my last words, for this book. I give each one of you my love and blessing and hope that you may become ever more conscious of the presence and comfort of your own guides and guardian angels.

Exercises Relating to this Chapter

Guided Journey to the Estuary and the Sea Beyond

Sit or lie in a comfortable but symmetrically balanced position, and make sure that you will be undisturbed.

Have a blanket at hand for warmth, and crayons and paper for recording and drawing.

Be aware of the rhythm of your breathing . . . gradually bring that rhythm into your heart centre or chakra . . . Travel on the heart energy into your inner landscape . . . Find yourself in the meadow . . . Awaken your inner senses, so that you see the objects and colours around you . . . hear the sounds . . . smell the fragrances . . . touch the textures . . . and taste the savours . . . Ask for your inner wise presence to accompany you or to bless this journey . . . Make sure that you have with you any talisman or amulet you wish to take . . .

From the meadow take the path which leads to the landing-stage . . .

The landing-stage represents the place which you have reached in your life's voyage . . . The journey which you are about to undertake is to the place where your river joins the sea and from where your essence returns to the source . . . Before you board the boat for this journey, call to yourself a colour on which you can rise above the landscape of your river to a vantage point . . . Look back over the pattern of your river and remember the journeys you have already taken . . . From your discoveries in those journeys, what do you want to take forward? . . . What will you definitively leave behind? . . . (Stay at your vantage point for five to six minutes to consider these choices . . .)

Return, on your coloured light, from your vantage point . . . Ask your guardian angel to be behind you, enfolding its wings about you; ask also your inner wise presence and perhaps your power animal to be with you, and board your boat . . .

In the next ten minutes, take a slowly paced journey along the river and into the estuary . . . When you enter the estuary, your boat will be tethered or anchored at a point where you can safely contemplate the joining of the river with the sea . . .

As you look out to sea, review the experience and learning which will be imprinted on your essence when you cross the threshold into death . . . Focus on the gifts you have to take back to your soul stem with you . . . Make this review without false pride, but also without false modesty . . . When you come to the things you regret, try to be as gentle on yourself as those who meet us on the other side will be . . . (Remember Gildas's previous explanations of the love with which we are met) . . .

Continuing to look out to sea, imagine the joy of meeting with loved ones who have passed on before . . . What important things will you have to tell them? . . .

Notice now that there is a misty and gentle, but bright, light over the sea . . . Know that, when your boat eventually makes its final voyage for this life, you will be drawn into that light, and with it will return to your source . . .

Look into the light and tell the light your fears of death and dying . . . ask that a symbol of peace and comfort may come out of the light and into your heart . . . Open your heart to receive this symbol . . .

It is time now for your boat to return to the landing-stage . . . Take the journey slowly, as you did on the way down to the estuary, holding your symbol of comfort in your heart . . .

At the landing-stage, thank your companions for their presence . . . Return to the meadow . . . Remember that the meadow is a place of transition, so rest a while here, if you wish, before returning to the awareness of your breath in your heart centre . . . your body and its contact with the ground . . . and your everyday surroundings . . .

Put a cross of light in a circle of light over your heart

centre as a blessing, and gently fold the petals of your heart chakra around your symbol of peace . . . Encircle your whole body with a cloak of light and a hood of light . . .

Take time to record and draw your journey . . .

Reflections on Your Journey

In this journey the reflections are built in, and there are no special questions to ask about them. Record this journey in a meditative way, continuing the reflections already begun.

Imagine Your Funeral or Life Celebration after You Are Dead

Plan how you would like your funeral to be. Whom would you wish to be present? Do you want to be buried or cremated? If cremated, where would you like your ashes to be scattered?

What sort of music and readings would you like at the service? Would you invite any particular person to speak? Where would you like the service to be? How would you like people to be dressed? Do you want flowers, or would you like to ask people to give a donation to your favourite charity, or to plant some trees in your memory?

What would you like to have written about you on your memorial stone?

Contemplate the Process of Your Dying

Supposing that your death is not sudden, how would you like your last weeks or days to be? Who would you like with you? What colours would you wish to have around you?

What goodbyes do you need to say? What affairs do you need to put in order? Are there things to say to people, letters to write, which you know you will regret not having said or written before you die?

As the moment of your death approaches, would you like silent comfort from loved ones? Would you like music to be played, or poetry read? Would you like to be alone? Is there someone you might ask to be with you, in those hours, who could remind you of the presence of your guardian angels and guides?

What instructions would you like to leave for the care of your body after death? Have you thought about whether you want your body used for medical research or not? Do you want to be cremated or buried? (This question is asked again here, so that you can be clear about it and give the appropriate instructions.)

As a result of your reflections, consider formally writing down your wishes concerning your death, and read them through together with a loved one who is likely to be close to you when you die. Seal the instructions into an envelope and make sure that they will be accessible, and remembered, when you are nearing death.

THINGS THAT GILDAS HAS SAID IN THE PAST ABOUT CARE OF THE DYING AND THE BODY AFTER DEATH

1. Except in very hot climates, try to leave at least three days between death and burial or cremation. During this time the full transition to the subtle, afterlife body is made. Certain essences required in the afterlife are withdrawn from the

physical body and its organs. (In hot climates the whole process is quicker, but an interval of twelve hours is desirable.)

2. After three days, your body is an empty shell and can be buried, cremated or given for medical research.

3. Gildas does see a problem with the donation of vital living organs. He is not in favour of transplants, with the exception of bone marrow, blood transfusions and corneas.

4. If possible, have friends to watch over your body for the three essential days and nights. Ideally the body should be surrounded by flowers, light colours, natural light and lighted candles. Rosemary and lavender fragrances and the playing of baroque music help during this transition period.

Case History: The Estuary and the Sea Beyond

Melanie had cancer of the lymph system. She had de-cided against chemotherapy or radiation and was work-ing with diet, counselling, homoeopathy, acupuncture and visualisation. Her life had been one of considerable mate-rial deprivation, though she had managed to buy a small flat after her parents died and she had some money left to her by a distant relative, which she was resolutely saving for 'a rainy day'.

At first she insisted that she was working towards a cure for the cancer, that she felt happy with life and was getting insights into the life factors which had contributed to her illness.

One day I asked her, intuitively but directly: 'Do you honestly want the outcome of this illness to be life or death?'

Melanie accepted the question calmly, and after a few moments of silence said: 'I have known for some time that what I really want is death. I am tired of fighting, but I thought I had to go on doing so because it was expected of me.'

We then talked about her present quality of life. She was still doing some work as a temporary secretary. She found her flat dark and cramped and did not really like the area it was in or its atmosphere. She longed to paint, draw, cook and sew beautiful fabrics – things for which she had rarely had time, space or energy.

Melanie asked the doctor who was supporting her management of her illness how long she would have to live if she stopped even her 'complementary' therapies. The estimate was six to nine months.

Since bringing her wish to die out into the open, Melanie had looked better and had more energy. She decided that it was time to make her rainy day into a sunny one. She sold her meagre little flat and rented one with large rooms, including a lovely kitchen. The aspect was sunny, with a view of gardens and trees.

She bought paints, pastels and paper, some lovely fabrics, a large tapestry and bright wools. Melanie spent her days painting, drawing, sewing and resting. She cooked lovely meals for her friends. As she began to get weaker, these same friends formed rotas to be with her and look after her. It was a pleasure to do so, since Melanie had created such a lovely atmosphere and was content in herself.

Melanie died as she had wished to die, with one close friend beside her. Her body was accompanied for three days and nights. She was surrounded by lighted candles, music and fragrance. Melanie had described her cremation service as a 'valedictory service of blessing'. All who attended wore bright colours and brought wild flowers to lay on her coffin. The service included readings from Kahlil Gibran's *The Prophet* and the playing of arias from Melanie's favourite operas. We were all very moved to receive personal gifts and cards, which Melanie had prepared well in advance.

Dying gracefully and consciously had become Melanie's life work. Her passing left a deep impression on all who were involved.

Glossary

Alchemy: A tradition which originated in Persia. In Europe, in the Middle Ages, alchemists were seen as being engaged on research which would enable lead, (base metal), to be transformed into gold. Undoubtedly some, usually called 'puffers and blowers', undertook such research. The true spiritual alchemy uses the imagery of base metal being transformed into gold as a basis for complex esoteric teaching about the journey and evolution of the soul.

Angels: (*See also Chapter 5.*) Angels are direct reflections of divine consciousness. They are intermediaries and guardians helping the divine plan to manifest on earth.

The elemental/devic/angelic hierarchy or lifestream may be seen as moving from the divine consciousness towards earth, while the human stream of consciousness, which includes discarnate guides, may be seen to be moving towards reunification with the divine. Thus the elemental/devic/angelic hierarchy is separate from humanity. Discarnates are not angels and angels will not take on human form or consciousness. Our guardian angels are different from our discarnate guides and mentors. (*See also 'Guardian angels'.*)

Altered state (of consciousness): Electrical cycles in the brain can be measured. When we are dealing with everyday functioning and the material world, there is a 'normal' range of cycles, known as the 'beta' rhythms. When we sleep, we are mainly in 'theta' rhythm. When, in waking consciousness, we are being particularly creative, 'alpha' rhythms may be present. Through meditation or hypnosis we may enter 'altered' states, in which beta rhythms fade, whilst alpha, delta and theta rhythms become more constant. In such states our physical bodies relax, we are more open to healing and we may have an expanded awareness in which the barriers of time and space are lessened.

Drugs may also induce altered states, but the cumulative side effects, and other factors which often accompany drug-taking, make them undesirable and usually counter-productive in any serious spiritual exploration.

Archetypes: By dictionary definition these are 'primordial images inherited by all'. Each human society is affected by forces such as peace, war, beauty, justice, wisdom, healing, death, birth, love, power. (These are sometimes called the **archetypes of higher qualities**.) The essence of these defies definition and we need images, myths, symbols and personifications to help us in understanding their depth and breadth. Tarot cards, which have ancient origins, have twenty-two personified or symbolised archetypes in the major arcana. These cover all aspects of human experience.

Astral plane: (*See 'Other planes'.*)

Aura: The energy field, which interpenetrates with, and radiates out beyond, the physical body. Clairvoyantly seen, the aura is full of light, colour and shade. The trained healer or seer sees or senses indications within the aura as to the spiritual, mental, physical and emotional state of the individual. Much of the auric colour and energy comes from the chakras.

Chakras: The word 'chakrum' is Sanskrit and means 'wheel'. Properly speaking, chakrum is the singular form and chakra the plural but in the West it is usual to speak of one chakra and many chakras. Much of the colour and energy of the auric field is supplied by the chakras. Clairvoyantly seen, they are wheels of light and colour interpenetrating with, affecting and affected by, the physical body. Most chakras carry links to specific parts of the glandular system and might therefore be described as subtle glands. Most Eastern traditions describe a sevenfold major chakra system, at the same time acknowledging varying large numbers of minor chakras throughout the body. The names of the major chakras are: the Crown (at the crown of the head); the Brow (above and between the eyes); the Throat (at the centre of the neck); the Heart (in the centre of the body, on the same level as the physical heart); the Solar Plexus (just under the rib cage); the Sacral (two fingers below the navel); and the Root (in the perineum area).

Chakras from the Solar Plexus upwards are often referred to as 'higher chakras' and the ones below and including the Solar Plexus as 'lower chakras'. These should not be seen as terms of evaluation. They are descriptive of the position of the chakras in relationship to the physical body when upright. There is not a hirarchical system within the chakras, each is part of a team.

There is a central subtle column of energy interpenetrating with the physical body and running from the crown of the head to the perineum (the area mid-way between the anus and the genitals). Each chakra has petals and a stem. The stems of the Crown and Root chakras are open and are contained within the central column. The other chakras have petals opening into the auric field at the front and stems at the back. The stems usually stay closed but the petals are flexible, opening and closing, vibrating and turning according to the different life situations encountered. A healthy chakra is a flexible chakra. Where there is disease, the chakra energies become inflexible or actually blocked. Working with chakras can thus aid physical, mental, emotional and spiritual health.

The seven major chakras carry the colours of the rainbow spectrum: red for the Root; orange for the Sacral; yellow for the Solar Plexus; green for the Heart; blue for the Throat; indigo for the Brow and violet for the Crown. This does not neccessarily mean that the chakras *are* these colours, but that they are responsible for that colour note within the chakra team and the auric field. Any colour may be 'seen' or sensed in *any* chakra. It could be said that each chakra has its own full spectrum of colour. The presence, quality and degree of other colours reflects information about ourselves.

Colours and their symbolism: There are seven colours in the basic 'rainbow' spectrum: **red; orange; yellow; green; blue; indigo; violet.** The chakra colours correspond to this spectrum. (*See above*). In terms of measurable vibrations, **red** is the lowest colour on the scale and **violet** the highest.

In life, we make many associations to colours. Each one has its positive and negative aspects.

Thus on the positive side: **red** is for warmth, life – force, energy, passion and celebration; **orange** is for vitality, initiation, creativity and sexuality; **yellow** is for light, springtime, new beginnings, clarity and joy; **green** is for growth, peace, restfulness and compassion; **blue** is for coolness, royalty, prayer, communication and healing; **indigo and violet** are for richness, ritual, spirituality and achievement.

On the negative side: **red** is for danger, anger, wounding and desecration; **orange** is for violence, aggression, negative power and destruction; **yellow** is for criticism, cowardice, tawdriness and loss of hope; **green** is for jealousy, bitterness, misfortune and poisoning; **blue** is for coldness, cruelty, death and deterioration; **indigo and violet** are for aloofness, misuse of power and loss of hope.

Black is the absorption of all colours. Positively it means dignity, mourning, the unknown, elegance, incubation and containment. Negatively it is evil, nightmare, rape, death and the void.

White is the reflection of all colours. Positively it means innocence, virginity, freshness, neutrality, grace and divinity. Negatively it is blankness, harshness, shallowness and cowardly surrender.

Silver and gold are the colours of the sun and moon. Traditionally silver represents the feminine principle and gold the masculine.

On the positive side, **silver** stands for cleansing, gentle strength, purity, natural rhythms, ebb and flow, mirroring, reflection and vision. On the negative side it is coldness, harshness, rigidity and treachery.

Positively, **gold** is abundance, the divine, high spiritual attainment, warmth, harmony and perfection. Negatively it represents materialism, opulence, false values and false images.

Pink, when positive, means love, tenderness, romance, birth, childlikeness and fragrance. Negatively it means faint-heartedness, childishness, lack of taste and artificiality.

Brown has the positive attributes of fertility, containment, seedtime, harvest and mellowness. Negatively it represents blockage, filth, obstacles, depression and despair.

Sometimes the difference between the positive and negative side of a colour is experienced in the shade or tone. At other times only the person who has the colour as a symbol will know, from its context and from what is happening in their lives, whether it has a positive or negative meaning for them. All meanings should be seen as messages which bring clarity and choice, not as portents.

Devic beings: These may sometimes be confused with angels. Devas are good, shining spirits, often perceived as being very tall. Their concern is with trees, rocks, plants, animals and the four elements. They are guardians who work to maintain balance in these realms and in the interaction of humanity with the natural kingdoms.

Discarnates (guides): Technically the term discarnate applies to any being or intelligence which is not in a physical body and incarnate on planet earth. In this book it is used to refer to guides and helpers from other planes, who are part of the human stream of consciousness but, at present, not in incarnation. Such guides have reached a point where their evolution is continuing without the need to reincarnate.

Elementals: Tiny energy beings generally associated with plants, trees, the natural environment and the elements. They appear to those who 'see', as points of light or colour or in traditional fairy form as the nereids, sylphs, gnomes, elves, undines, goblins and flower fairies.

Since the four elements interact in our physical bodies and largely determine our health patterns, elementals are within and around us. The giving and receiving of energetic healing activates and encourages them to help us to health and harmony.

Elementals are the lowest manifestation in a hierarchy of a different consciousness stream from the human. Above them are devic beings and angels.

Fairies: *(See 'Elementals' above.)*

Feeling plane: *(See 'Other planes'.)*

Findhorn Foundation: A long-established spiritual community at Findhorn in Scotland. They run courses and retreats and produce a number of spiritual cards, games and other publications.

Guardian angel: We each have a guardian angel who watches over us from before birth and accompanies our passage through death. Our guardian angel evolves from the elemental hierarchy to accompany us on our journey when our soul decides to take on another incarnation. When we die our guardian angel moves on to some other angelic task. *(See also 'Angels'.)*

Higher self: Our higher self is, in essence, the part of our consciousness or soul which does not incarnate. The higher self has an overview of all our lifetimes and decides our task and purpose in each incarnation.

Karma: The spiritual law of cause and effect (which defies 'nut-shell' definition). 'As you sow, so shall you reap', gives a basic but over-simplified idea. Belief in karma goes alongside belief in reincarnation and personal, progressive evolution. The tendency is to see karma as being something troublesome or heavy which needs to be overcome during a specific lifetime – but giftedness or innate wisdom are positive karmic attributes.

Mental plane: *(See 'Other planes'.)*

Other planes: When incarnate, our existence is dependent upon the material plane where things have substance and solidity. Yet we are complex beings and if we pause to study the range of our perceptions, not all can be explained by the laws of physics. Many people encounter 'other-worldly phenomena', from near-death experiences to prophetic dreams, from sensing 'atmospheres' in old buildings to telepathic communication with a loved one, either alive or dead.

Esoteric teaching tells us that there are at least six other planes of experience, which are not just phenomena of perception but actual territories. The nearest to us is the etheric plane, which in itself is largely an interface between the material and the astral planes. This latter is divided into a number of layers or regions. The lower astral is largely populated with negative thought forms. (It is probably the region which severe alcoholics experience when they have DTs or drug users when they have a 'bad trip'.) The higher levels of the astral plane are where we meet our guides, where there are temples of light and healing and beautiful, subtle landscapes. We may visit the astral planes in our dreams, each night, as well as being able to travel there in the altered state of consciousness induced by meditation. Beyond the astral plane are the feeling plane, the lower and higher mental planes and the causal plane. (Names for each of the planes may vary from teacher to teacher, those used here are as given by Gildas.)

Projection: A complex psychological mechanism – again defying 'nutshell' definition – whereby we disown, or are unconscious of our own behaviours and needs but reflect them on to others who have the necessary 'hook'. Thus, at the basic and most simplistic level, a motherly looking woman may find others expecting her to mother them – and being 'blamed' or causing anger when she does not do so; a powerfully built man may attract projections of either 'the hero' or 'the brute'.

Projections account for many of the difficulties and misunderstandings which arise in human relationships.

Psyche: Analytic and transpersonal psychologies have shown how complex the human personality is. The psyche refers to the total being, with all its drives, needs, conflicts, disease, health, gifts and potential.

Shadow: The part of the 'I' which we do not admit into full consciousness. That which is unconscious, undefined, formless, dark, shadowy and without concept. The unknown.

Shamanism: A tradition which originated in Iceland and parts of Russia. It is also practised by the North and South American Indians. Shamans undergo rigorous training which enables them to become seers and healers and to cross the boundaries between the planes, in full consciousness. Neo-shamanism is a re-awakening of the shamanic tradition.

Soul (also soul thread, soul family and soul group):
Here I quote Gildas:

'The original spark or soul comes from the Source. In order to become like the Source the soul takes on incarnation and journeys through many lifetimes, in search of evolution. Gradually an oversee-ing, observing or higher self, emerges. Then each time incarnation takes place only a part of the whole becomes personified in order to undergo the further experience which the essence requires in its search for wholeness.

'The essence or soul thread is vital, increasingly conscious and eternal. The learning process continues on other planes of being, between as well as during lifetimes.

'Souls belong to families and groups. Let me paint you a picture: First, imagine a tree, then the forest in which it stands, then many other forests of trees. Twigs, leaves and fruits which spring from the same branch are soul families. Branches on the same tree are soul groups, forests are wider soul groups.'

Rite of passage: At certain moments in our lives, we move definitively from one stage to the next. Puberty declares that child-hood is over, we are sexually mature and capable of procreation; 'coming of age' marks our entry into adult responsibilities within our culture; marriage signifies that we are ready for family responsi-bilities of our own. Birth and death are great 'mysteries', but also mark the passage from one state of being to another. Rites of passage are the rituals, initiations and celebrations which accompany our crossing of each threshold.

Recommended Reading

Cooper, C. J., *An Illustrated Encyclopaedia of Symbols*, Thames and Hudson

Jung, C. J., *Man and His Symbols*, Aldus Books

Claremont di Castiliego, Catherina, *Knowing Woman*, Shambhala Publications

Burckhardt, Titus, *Alchemy*, Element Books

Krystall, Phylliss, *Cutting the Ties that Bind*, Weiser

Reinhart, Melanie, *Chiron and the Healing Journey*, Arkana

LeShan, Lawrence, *How to Meditate*, Aquarian

Cade, M. & Coxhead, N., *The Awakened Mind*, Element Books

Mitchell, Waldorf M., *Complexity*, Penguin

Adams, Jeremiah, *Reclaiming the Inner Child*, Mandala

Books by Ruth White
(The first three titles are all written with Mary Swainson.)
Gildas Communicates, C. W. Daniel Co Ltd
Seven Inner Journeys, C. W. Daniel Co Ltd
The Healing Spectrum, C. W. Daniel Co Ltd
A Question of Guidance, C. W. Daniel Co Ltd
Working With Your Chakras, Piatkus Books
A Message of Love, Piatkus Books
Working with Guides and Angels, Piatkus Books
Chakras: A New Approach to Healing Your Life, Piatkus Books

Index